A Future and a Hope

The story of Tearfund, and why God wants
the church to change the world

A Future and a Hope

THE STORY OF TEARFUND, AND WHY GOD WANTS THE CHURCH TO CHANGE THE WORLD

MIKE HOLLOW

MONARCH
BOOKS

Oxford, UK, and Grand Rapids, Michigan, USA

First published in the UK in 2008 by Monarch Books
(a publishing imprint of Lion Hudson plc),
Wilkinson House, Jordan Hill Road, Oxford OX2 8DR
Tel: +44 (0) 1865 302750   Fax: +44 (0) 1865 302757
Email: monarch@lionhudson.com
www.lionhudson.com

Co-published with Tearfund
100 Church Road, Teddington TW11 8QE
Tel: +44 (0) 20 8977 914

Distributed by:
UK: Marston Book Services Ltd, PO Box 269, Abingdon, Oxon OX14 4YN.
USA: Kregel Publications, PO Box 2607, Grand Rapids, Michigan 49501.

ISBN: 978-1-85424-865-7 (UK)
ISBN: 978-0-8254-6197-2 (USA)

The text paper used in this book has been made from wood
independently certified as having come from sustainable forests.

British Library Cataloguing Data
A catalogue record for this book is available from the British Library.

Printed and bound in China.

This book is dedicated to all those who have supported

Tearfund with their prayer, action and

giving over the last forty years,

without whom the story could not be told.

Photo Credits

Peter Caton/Tearfund: 196.
Geoff Crawford/Tearfund: 20, 31, 75, 79, 100, 139, 140, 184, 193.
Gordon Davies/Tearfund: 71.
EFICOR: 174.
Richard Hanson/Tearfund: 68, 69, 73, 105, 106, 122, 123, 143, 158,
162, 172, 200, 216.
Mike Hollow/Tearfund: 72.
Caroline Irby/Tearfund: 61, 77, 78, 84.
Jim Loring/Tearfund: 15, 19, 42, 57, 74, 86, 101, 102, 109, 111, 114,
118, 131, 141, 146, 148, 150, 160, 187, 195, 197, 198, 201, 202,
205, 206, 208, 215.
Alan Olley/Cliff Richard Organisation: 11.
Marcus Perkins/Tearfund: 33, 35, 52, 81, 82, 97, 113, 116, 121, 124,
145, 166, 210, 213.
Esther Stansfield/Tearfund: 189.
Tearfund: 13, 17, 26, 27, 28, 34, 39, 41, 43, 44, 50, 53, 55, 59, 60,
63, 64, 67, 80, 88, 90, 92, 94, 96, 119, 127, 129, 130, 134, 135, 136,
138, 147, 153, 155, 156, 159, 173, 177, 178.
Layton Thompson/Tearfund: 65, 165, 188, 192.
Mike Webb/Tearfund: 18, 99, 103, 157, 168, 169, 179.

Contents

Preface

To be asked to write the story of Tearfund was a privilege, and it also proved to be a huge pleasure. There are so many exciting stories, so many remarkable people in so many places, I could have written three or four more. Inevitably, I feel as though I have barely skimmed the surface of all that's happened since Tearfund started. For every person quoted in these pages there are dozens more whose stories I could have told. For every project mentioned there are scores doing equally effective work.

I am grateful to all those who have shared with me their memories and insights, which were always helpful and often inspiring. My thanks go to everyone who helped me in other ways too many to mention, both inside and outside Tearfund.

I can only hope that I have captured something of the passion, excitement and vision that has fuelled Tearfund's growth and achievement over the years, and the potential it has for the future. My 'expert witnesses' who have lived through the story of those years assure me that this account is faithful, but of course any factual inaccuracies are mine.

Mike Hollow

Foreword
Sir Cliff Richard OBE

Little did I think that the fundraising concert I gave at the Royal Albert Hall way back in 1968 would mark the start of a nearly forty-year relationship with Tearfund. It's been a relationship that has cost me relatively little but has given me a thousand-fold back.

I was a very naive, but hungry, young Christian at the start of it all. For two or three years, I'd grappled in my head with Jesus' claims and teaching. It resulted in an earnest commitment to Christ. But then what? I needed to *do* something as a Christian. I had a responsibility; I'd read the Scripture that 'from everyone who has been given much, much will be demanded'. Much had been given to me, that was for sure.

And then Tearfund came into my life. It was so obvious. Christians had to demonstrate God's love, and the world so badly needed it. There were stories about aid agencies wasting money on help that was irrelevant or inappropriate. Grain was left rotting on quaysides; money was being siphoned off by corrupt officials. And there was Tearfund, offering me the opportunity to come alongside Christians in desperately needy places, enabling them to do a better job. Medics, engineers, agriculturalists – all offering their skills and experience where it was relevant, and doing it in the name of Jesus.

It wasn't long before I made my first overseas trip with Tearfund. It was to Bangladesh and it was grim. I'd never seen poverty, pain and anguish like it, and I felt guilty at leaving and returning to my pop-star lifestyle. The admonition of one wise nurse set me straight and her words have rung in my ears ever since: 'Go home and do what you're good at!'

Whether I'm good at anything is a matter of conjecture, but it's been a privilege and a joy to be linked with an organisation that God has blessed so mightily over these four decades. My visits to aid programmes in Uganda, Sudan, Haiti, Nepal and Cambodia have confirmed for me beyond any doubt that Tearfund's input is not only fruitful, but reflects the very heart of the Christian gospel. Far from being downcast or pessimistic, I've always returned from those trips personally inspired and encouraged by what I've encountered. In my rarefied world of showbiz, it's not always easy to spot acts of self-giving love. Dip into Tearfund and you'll find it by the bucket-load – and it works wonders for your faith!

And the joy? There's been plenty of that too. The series of gospel concert tours that I was able to perform in aid of Tearfund – mainly in the 1970s, 80s and 90s – was another example of the church joining forces to achieve something good. Money was raised, Christians were blessed, and some found Jesus for the first time.

At the beginning, there was but a scattering of Tearfund supporters and helpers. Today they are legion. They pray, they offer their time and they give their money – not once but regularly, again and again. The great majority of these folk won't have the opportunity to see the fruit of their generosity and obedience, but you can take it from me that the fruit is there and the fruit will last.

I forgot to mention – the aim of that concert at the Royal Albert Hall in 1968 was to raise the princely sum of £1,500. It was enough to buy a Land Rover for use in South America. I guess today it might just be enough to cover the cost of the tyres!

Foreword
Lord Carey of Clifton

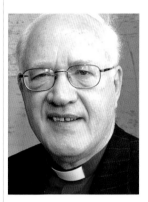

When I became Archbishop of Canterbury in 1991 I had never travelled to the developing world. Then I visited Africa, and experienced the range of emotions that hit any of us when we're exposed to global poverty. The first emotion is anger: you feel really angry at the unfairness of life and what we have. The second is shame: you feel ashamed that you've neglected this area all this time, that the knowledge was around but you've missed it. The third is guilt: I should have done something about it. Finally comes a feeling of hopelessness: the needs are so vast – what can I do about it?

For me, the turning point came when I visited southern Sudan in 1993. I vowed that from that moment on I would talk and preach about development. I am convinced that we have to translate word into action – we have to translate the gospel we preach into the gospel we live and act.

That's why when my wife Eileen and I were invited to become Vice-Presidents of Tearfund, we accepted enthusiastically. We feel very privileged to be part of Tearfund's work. I was a close friend of Tearfund's founding director George Hoffman in the 1950s, and when Tearfund started in 1968 I welcomed it wholeheartedly.

As an evangelical Christian I was committed to mission in its fullest sense. I deplored the way many of my generation spiritualised the gospel: suggesting the most important thing is preaching to the soul, the body looks after itself, and if it doesn't then God's got a place for you in heaven. To me, that kind of theology was a distortion, and Tearfund seemed to be taking up again the historical evangelical legacy of concern for the poor.

Tearfund is quite categorically gospel-centred, and that makes its contribution very valuable indeed. It has become a credible and respected mainstream relief and development agency, but has remained thoroughly Christian in its approach, keeping faith with the ethics of Jesus. It is this continuing Christian commitment that makes Tearfund so distinctive.

As I've travelled, I've also seen the strength of Tearfund's work with the local church. Tearfund is perhaps unique in that it's mobilising the biggest grass-roots army of committed workers in the world: the ordinary men and women of the church. This dedicated network of power and care could transform the world – and transformation is what the gospel is all about.

Supporting Tearfund has become a regular feature of the life of many churches, and this can bring an unexpected blessing. When Tearfund becomes a significant element in a local church's life, it has the potential – I've seen it happen again and again – to really invigorate the church itself for mission. Giving to Tearfund reminds us of what the gospel is all about, and it brings fresh impetus to the work of the church here.

Tearfund began as a miracle, an idea that took root in the minds of a small group of Christian people, and forty years later it has grown into something with enormous potential. What God has done among us is simply stupendous.

The story of Tearfund is an inspiring story of what God is doing in the world. I hope that as you read this book you too will be inspired with a vision of how much more he wants to do through his people: you and me.

Introduction

'**T**he poor,' said Jesus, 'you will always have with you.' There was a time – and perhaps still is – when for some Christians this meant poverty is here to stay and there's nothing we can do about it. Worse, these words in Matthew 26:11 would be quoted as a justification for remaining passive in a world of crying need. But Jesus was quoting the Bible – Deuteronomy 15:11, to be precise. Among the commands God gave to his people through Moses was this: 'There will always be poor people in the land. Therefore I command you to be open-handed towards those of your people who are poor and needy in your land.'

The story of Tearfund is part of a bigger story: how God has awoken a fresh understanding of this compassion among Christians in the British Isles since the mid-twentieth century. In particular, it's about how the Holy Spirit worked in evangelical Christians to re-energise their concern for social as well as spiritual needs.

Tearfund came into existence because evangelical Christians wanted to do something about suffering in the world – and to do it in the name of Jesus. The growth of Tearfund over the last forty years is evidence of a change: an increasing desire to engage with the Bible's challenge on poverty and justice, and to be open-handed towards the poor and needy people of the world.

It started with a handful of people sitting round a table in London in 1968. To their surprise, it grew beyond all expectations. A vision swept through the church. Individuals, families and churches gave their money, their time and their prayer to help people around the world find the fullness of life that Jesus talked about.

A new understanding began to emerge: that Christians did not have to choose between proclamation of the gospel and social action as if these were two conflicting brands of faith. Instead, bringing good news to the poor, as Jesus did, meant an integrated life of truth and action. Through Tearfund, Christians in the UK discovered the experience of churches in poorer parts of the world that made this concept a visible reality. Now, we can see in every part of our own country churches taking this integral vision of the gospel to people in need on their own doorstep.

In 1968 this was a radical message. The fact that for today's generation it is a normal part of Christian discipleship is testimony to the extraordinary effect Tearfund has had on the church, and how God has worked in and through Tearfund to change and enlarge the church's vision for the impact of the gospel on the world.

Through its struggles, successes and failures of the last forty years, Tearfund has learnt how to bring emergency relief and long-term development to places of poverty and suffering in a distinctively Christian way, with a mission to the whole person. It has enabled thousands of local church-based groups in developing countries to proclaim their faith in both word and deed, in ways that show the gospel is truly good news. It has inspired a movement of Christians in the UK and other western nations to adopt a lifestyle that puts their faith into action.

Yes, the poor are still with us, as Jesus said they would be – but through the work of Tearfund and the compassion of God's people worldwide, many of them can now say that they have truly found a future and a hope.

Chapter 1

New Face

1968: a tumultuous year to be born. 'Revolution' was the Beatles song that topped the charts, but it wasn't just about a song: moral and political revolution was in the air and on the streets. In France, May 1968 saw students and anarchists taking to the streets in riots that threatened to bring down the government. All of Europe watched nervously.

The birth of Tearfund was hardly likely to be noticed against such a dramatic backdrop. But not for the first time, while the world's eyes were focused on the politics of power, God was doing something unseen, unacknowledged. A mustard seed was germinating, and soon it would break the surface and begin to grow.

On the evening of 29 May, even those who weren't preoccupied with politics had their attention elsewhere. At Wembley Stadium, Manchester United were playing Benfica in the European Cup Final, and their 4-1 victory made them the first English team ever to win the trophy.

In another part of London, however, at the Evangelical Alliance headquarters in Bloomsbury, a handful of people had gathered for the first meeting of a new body: the less than excitingly named Evangelical Alliance Relief Fund Committee, which in time would become known as Tearfund. They were accountant Glyn Macaulay, university administrator John Boxhall, missionary leader Ernest Oliver, former Church of England curate George Hoffman, graphic designer Peter Meadows and student Mary Jean Duffield.

Also with them was the man whose idea it had been to bring them together: Morgan Derham, who had become General Secretary of the Evangelical Alliance two years earlier. With a vision to see evangelical Christians more involved in alleviating global poverty, he'd hired Mary Jean in January 1967 to be his researcher for the year before she started her course at the London School of Economics. As she

Morgan Derham, General Secretary of the Evangelical Alliance, brought together the small team that would get Tearfund off the ground.

Aid for Jordan Refugees

AT THE TIME of writing we are organising a scheme for sending clothes and other gifts to Jordan for refugee needs there. Mr. and Mrs. Howard Norrish, who have had to return from missionary service in Jordan, are responsible for the scheme, with the backing of a small committee of experienced people. Full details of what is needed and of the address to which supplies should be sent will be available from EA headquarters very soon. In the meantime, gifts of money for the same purpose may be sent to the EA Relief Fund, 30 Bedford Place, London, W. C. 1.

Tearfund's first appeal for funds – for refugees in Jordan. It was published in the Summer 1967 issue of the Evangelical Alliance *Broadsheet*.

When famine, war or other disasters drive people from their homes, it is the most vulnerable – children, women, the elderly – who suffer most. Tearfund began with simple acts of compassion for refugees.

recalled later, her job was to investigate the potential for an evangelical relief fund:

> Tearfund started with Morgan Derham's vision. If he hadn't been there it wouldn't have happened. He was such a whole person, with a vision for the whole of life. He gave me a muddled stack of miscellaneous missionary magazines and said, 'Go and have a look at those and see what we could do.'
>
> There was just a complete mixture and a lot of it was completely irrelevant, but I do remember we found something about the refugees in Amman, Jordan, and that became our first appeal. Amman was our first advertisement, which I did on the desk in between deciding where I was going to go that evening.

This meeting was the formal starting point for Tearfund, but in fact the story goes back further: to 1960, when World Refugee Year highlighted the needs of the estimated 40 million people around the world who had been forced from their homes by war and disaster. Before the visionary actions of any one man, the origins of Tearfund lay in a spontaneous move of compassion among British Christians. Gifts of money and goods began to arrive at the Evangelical Alliance (EA), with requests that they be used to help suffering refugees. Glyn Macaulay, who would later become Tearfund's first chairman, serving until 1975, recalled those days:

> Many Christians were concerned that money given should not be lost in world systems, governments, the World Council of Churches and the like. Other agencies such as Oxfam and Save the Children did good work but were not Christian. The evangelical community was starting to sense that there was a need, to such an extent that the hallway in the EA office in Bedford Place was rapidly getting cluttered with piles of clothing, baby food and so on. Christians were saying to the EA, 'Here is my donation; please do something about it.'
>
> So the EA was asking itself, 'Do we pursue this?' There was a strong sense that

The name

It started as the Evangelical Alliance Relief Fund, and in 1968 the acronym TEAR Fund was adopted. In the early years, the organisation's own publicity referred to it variously as Tear Fund and TEAR Fund, even within the same publication, before settling on Tear Fund from 1978. For the first eighteen years the 'small print' of the organisation's logo continued to spell out the full version of the name, but this was dropped in 1986, when a new corporate identity and logo were adopted. The word 'Tear' ceased to stand for 'The Evangelical Alliance Relief Fund', and since then it has simply been a name in its own right. In 1998 it became one word: Tearfund.

evangelicals would support an organisation that made it very clear it would only work through Christians in the developing world – not giving aid money only to Christians, but making sure it would go from Christians here in the UK to Christians in the developing world who would use it to bring help to anyone in need, whatever religious belief they might have.

What to do with this money? In January 1960 the Alliance's Executive Council passed a recommendation:

> In response to numerous requests the Evangelical Alliance should set up a fund whereby gifts from churches and individuals may be distributed to evangelical agencies in different parts of the world that are engaged in caring for the material and spiritual needs of refugees.

For Christians who recognised their responsibility to help meet the needs of the hungry, Tearfund was the obvious way to give.

This recommendation was ratified on 25 February, and the Evangelical Alliance's Refugee Fund came into being. Its resources were small, just £635, but it set about making grants, the first being to provide care for refugees in Hong Kong. Over its first year the fund received donations totalling £2,687, and as the 1960s went by it continued to receive donations and to disburse money. From the start the purpose of the fund was clear, as expressed, for example, in the Winter 1963 issue of the Evangelical Alliance *Broadsheet*:

Whether it's earthquake, flood, famine or war – or, as here, in the wake of the devastating tsunami of 2004 in Sri Lanka – providing emergency relief in time of disaster is as important to Tearfund today as it was at the beginning.

Refugee fund

A less spectacular part of the Alliance's work, but one which we believe to be most vital, has not been neglected during the year. We refer to the Refugee and Bursary (Scholarship) Funds. Over £7,000 has been distributed to evangelical Christians working amongst needy peoples and especially refugees, including £750 sent for disbursement by the Rt Rev Lawrence Barham, Bishop of Rwanda and former Vice-Chairman of the Evangelical Missionary Alliance, and £500 sent to Mr I Ben Wati to be used in India.

From the 'Survey of the Year' in the Evangelical Alliance Annual Report 1964

Moneys are still sent by churches and individuals to the Alliance to be distributed to evangelical missions and churches that are carrying on a work among refugees in different parts of the world. The Alliance is happy, and indeed privileged, to act as a steward in this way, and guarantees that such moneys go to those who are truly evangelical in their outlook, and whose work is felt worthy of the support of the Christian public.

After seven years of low-profile activity, there was a significant change of gear when in 1967 Morgan Derham hired George Hoffman to work as his assistant. This young man had been a curate in Edgware and for some months had been working on *Crusade* magazine. Morgan Derham assigned him a number of projects to work on, one of which was the fund, by now renamed the Relief Fund. Mary Jean later recalled:

> When George took over it moved into a different league. He had a great sense of giving the fund an identity and he relaunched it, as it were. I remember him saying that we had set it up, and for him it was like playing a golf ball off the tee.

> **I**f any one of you has material possessions and sees a brother or sister in need but has no pity on them, how can the love of God be in you? Dear children, let us not love with words or tongue but with actions and in truth. (1 John 3:17–18)

George Hoffman had an aptitude for publicity, and the fund began to be promoted more creatively. The sober wording of earlier announcements gave way to a more provocative tone, as a leaflet produced in that year shows:

> Starving people, and sun-baked soil – areas of need which concern every Christian today. Hungry bodies are the urgent, the immediate need – there are millions of them in Kerala (India) alone.
>
> But barren fields are the long-term problem. Every day someone, somewhere, has to make the hard decision between using resources to meet the needs of the hungry hundreds today and those of the hungry thousands in five years' time; but for some there is no such choice – neither way is open.
>
> This is because many Christians care for neither of these needs. The

I have NO HOME NOR PARENTS

I live in Vietnam, India, Hong Kong and other places. Missionaries tell me about Jesus; how He loves me. They tell me also of other Christians in far away places. Because they're Christians, they love me too. Sometimes I eat food and wear clothes and sleep at night under shelters they help to provide for me. I stop feeling hungry. I stop shivering when it's dark. And somehow I feel they do care for me. Then I know again that Jesus loves me too.

If you would like us to help Christians, both nationals and missionaries meet the needs of children and needy families in these and other areas, please send your gifts to or write for full details of our worldwide projects to:

Evangelical Alliance Relief, 30 Bedford Place, London, WC1.

Photo: Save the children fund

Publicity for the EA Relief Fund was getting under way: two months before the first meeting of the Tearfund committee, this advert appeared in the 'Homes & Parents' supplement of *Crusade* magazine, March 1968 issue.

DA NANG

AND

SAIGON

are just two of the many places where the

EVANGELICAL ALLIANCE RELIEF FUND

is helping Christians, both national and missionaries, to feed the hungry and house the homeless

HELP US TO HELP THEM

SEND YOUR GIFT TO

"EAR", 30 BEDFORD PLACE,
LONDON, W.C.1

An early advert for 'EAR': this one appeared in *Crusade* magazine, June 1968.

world is next door, in these days of swift travel and instant crises, yet many of us live as if the hungry peoples occupied some undiscovered planet. Some hold back because they do not really care: others because they do not know how best to share what they have. This brochure is for both groups.

The leaflet called on Christians to learn more about world needs, to give and to pray. It also urged young Christians with professional skills to put them to use in overseas service for the benefit of the poor. The canvas was beginning to broaden.

By the time the committee held its first meeting in May 1968, the Relief Fund had a sense of purpose and vision, as well as some modest funds. With the formation of the committee, however, it acquired a new energy: a team with a remarkable mix of personalities, skills and experience came together to drive it forward. Glyn Macaulay recalled:

> Mary Jean Duffield was a political animal and a real live wire; she came from a wealthy family, spoke her mind and was great value. Pete Meadows was the communicator, a PR man. John Boxhall, the university administrator, was very straight, very proper, very well dressed, everything was right about John. We had a very exciting mix of people round the table who had the enthusiasm to get things done: Mary Jean, who would have mortgaged everything to meet various needs, and George Hoffman, who was inclined that way too, but also the John Boxhalls and Glyn Macaulays of this world who would say, 'Wait just a minute,' and Pete Meadows, who was constantly looking for the promotional opportunity, to get something out as a prayer request, a newsletter item, a poster or whatever. They were exciting days.

Passion

❝ Tearfund passionately believes that God calls his people to meet the physical, spiritual and emotional needs of the poorest people. ❞

Tear Times, 2006

As Mary Jean would later recall, there was also a sense of this new initiative seizing the moment:

> I think if you start something like Tearfund it only works if the time is right and you strike a chord. As far as the Relief Fund was concerned, the time was right and it just caught on.

Give E.A.R.

❝ No, this is not just a bad pun; it marks a new stage in the development of the Evangelical Alliance's Relief Fund. A new unit has been set up at Headquarters, under Miss Mary-Jean Duffield, who is responsible to the General Secretary. This unit is co-ordinating the various fund-raising activities of the Alliance; in particular the Relief and Scholarship Funds.

The Relief Fund has been operating in relation to special cases of need as they have arisen; a gift was sent from it recently to assist evangelical pastors affected by the floods in Northern Italy. But the biggest concern in recent months has been Vietnam; and last month a gift of £1,000 was sent to the Evangelical Church there to help pastors and others who had become refugees or who had otherwise lost possessions or livelihood through the tragic war in that land.

India is another area of outstanding suffering; the Evangelical Fellowship of India has just set up a special Famine Relief Fund, and we shall be happy to arrange for money to be sent to help them in their great need, particularly in Bihar, where famine conditions cause widespread suffering.

In Africa, especially in the Congo, where the long task of rehabilitation goes on, we have direct links through the EMA societies, and can channel funds to where they will be directly related to evangelical life and service.

We are, therefore, putting a greater emphasis on our appeal fund, and advertising the need more widely – including by means of this *Broadsheet* paragraph, and would suggest that evangelical churches should direct their gifts through the EA fund; if your church does not at present have a regular scheme of giving to meet the needs of our brethren and sisters throughout the world, we suggest that you see that the matter is raised as soon as possible. ❞

Announcement in the Evangelical Alliance *Broadsheet*, Spring 1967

Before the fund could really take off, however, there was one small problem to solve: the name. Up to now, the Evangelical Alliance Relief Fund had been abbreviated to EAR, but this was not a viable basis for a higher profile. As Peter Meadows recalled, 'We had to do something about EAR Fund – it sounded like a mission to the deaf.' He raised the matter at the committee's second meeting, on 1 July 1968, and it was decided to adopt the name TEAR Fund.

It was Peter Meadows who also came up with the first logo. Myth has it that he hit upon the idea while doodling during a committee meeting, but the reality was different:

We needed a logo, and so because of my background in graphics, I was asked to create one. I did one saying EAR, and I looked at it and thought, no, we have to find another way. So in my studio I played with putting a T in front of it and thought, oh yes! I don't even know

Early Tearfund advertisements, from *Crusade* magazine in 1969. The use of full-page black-and-white adverts with a large, striking photograph and sparse text was a key element in Tearfund's style.

YOU CAN'T LIVE WITHOUT IT

A precious liquid called water.
Without it we die.
And in South India TEAR Fund is providing water for a score of villages through its first well boring scheme.

But more.
TEAR Fund also realises that men need the "Water of Life".
Without it, there is no true life.
That's why TEAR Fund is helping Evangelical Christians and missionaries who are ministering to both the physical and spiritual needs of all around them.

Maybe your Church or grou like to help.

Why not write for a poster details or send a gift to

30 BEDFORD PLA
LONDON WC1.

THE GAPING EARTH OF INDIA GASPS FOR WATER

TEAR Fund is helping with irrigation schemes and turning barrenness into fertility.

It is also concerned about the good seed of the Word falling into good ground.

Perhaps your Church or group could help, so why not write for details to:

TEAR FUND
The Evangelical Alliance Relief Fund

30 BEDFORD PLACE,
LONDON WC1.

TEAR TIMES

THE EVANGELICAL ALLIANCE RELIEF FUND

WINTER, 1973/74

Target exceeded for Chad: residue for Ethiopia

THERE has been a magnificent response by Christians throughout the country to Tear Fund's Christmas project for a water improvement programme in Chad, West Africa.

Virtually before Christmas, the target of £10,000 was in sight, and Eddie Smith, the Worldwide Evangelization Crusade missionary engineer, was given the go-ahead for his programme of well-digging and building of catchment tanks and reservoirs in villages where the nearest existing source of water is fifteen miles distant.

CLOSE LINK

The generous giving means that the present needs of this particular programme will be more than met. Money, therefore, received over and above the target and which is given as a direct result of the Christmas promotion, will be channelled to our emergency and long-term aid in Ethiopia. An outline of our projects there appear below and details are on Page 2.

The famine situation in Ethiopia is linked closely, of course, with conditions in Chad and those affecting the whole sub-Saharan belt.

ETHIOPIA

'I cried as I never cried before'

Youth Officer, Sarah Marrow, has recently returned from the famine areas of Ethiopia—her first overseas tour for Tear Fund. Here she recounts her feelings when the theory became people.

I STOOD and stared . . . I felt nothing. . . I couldn't cry . . . I couldn't speak . . . and I felt inadequate and helpless. Never in my life had I seen anything like it. Of course, in my job I'd seen endless pictures, I'd heard numerous talks, I'd led discussions, I'd learned statistics, and I'd even given talks myself about the third world; but what faced me at that moment in time, weren't pictures or statistics but people.

People unable to stand, unable to walk, lying in mud and filth; unable even to lift the food to their lips; people covered in torn, dirty rags; people crawling with fleas and lice; people with limbs like sticks; people with no homes, no possessions; people with malaria, dysentary, typhoid; people without hope – people suffering . . .

For a week I toured the famine area, I visited the camps, the orphanages, the clinics. I went out into the villages and flew over the drought-stricken areas and for a week I didn't want to talk about it. Then I cried . . . I cried as I've never cried before. I cried out of pity, and I cried out of anger. Anger at man's inhumanity to man, anger at all those

CLENCHED FISTS

"There have been those," she writes, who, standing in the midst of such scenes, have raised clenched fists to the brazen sky and cursed the

who've "walked by on the other side," the governments, the wealthy, the cynics, the landowners, the west and myself, because here 'people' created in the image of God were being degraded, humiliated, trampled on, and were dying in the mud. I suppose some might be angry at God, yet somehow I just shared the reactions of Rhena Taylor a B.C.M.S. missionary who volunteered to help in one of the feeding camps.

Creator, who allowed such suffering, such misery, such waste of life. But I could not do that. The God I had known through my youth, and now, had not changed overnight to being a cruel uncaring over lord. He had created man a being in His own image to enjoy the things of the earth, to be fruitful and multiply. If man had chosen his own way, if the earth had been abused, spoiled made worse; this was not God's fault.

"If my eyes wept at this sight, so more did His who taught me compassion. If I was crushed, bowed down by the weight of death and sickness, at seeing bodies twisted with the torment of hunger and thirst was He not also suffering? He who

taught me the value of soul and body."

These were the unlovely and unloved and of all people in this world, they need to be cared for, and shown the love of their Creator.

GO AND DO

Then I remembered the command of Jesus after describing the compassionate love of the good Samaritan – "Go and do thou likewise" – and that is not easy when it means 'go and live among the sick, the starving, the flea ridden, the dying – and love them in thought and deed'. Thank God some have gone and that the love of Jesus is being seen in action . . .

TEAR FUND'S ACTION— —SO FAR

£5,500
to Don Stilwell, Society of International Mission's famine relief co-ordinator: for food, medicines, blankets, mats and powdered milk.

£1,000
to Don Stilwell: for deepening and covering village wells.

£1,000
to Ken Radach S.I.M. missionary in charge of Alamatta relief centre: for sanitation and grain storage huts.

£1,000
to Bill Taylor a brethren missionary: for famine relief camps.

£500
to support Heather Bobbersmien S.R.N. a volunteer nurse working in Ethiopia for six months with the S.I.M. team.

—EARLY IN '74

APPROX.
£20,000
Halco 625 Drilling Rig: working with S.I.M. to sink wells in the famine areas (shared project with Christoffell Blinden Mission).

£3,500
Personnel :
a) support for short term volunteer nurses.
b) support for two engineers to man drilling rig.
(Both projects provisional at the time of going to Press)

Early issues of Tear Times *used large, stark photographs and a compelling writing style to capture the imagination of its readers – and to spark a compassionate response of prayer and giving.*

Tearfund's first leaders understood the power of the visual image – and used it to great effect.

where it came from. It came from outside somewhere, the way many good creative ideas come. Some ideas come from blood, sweat and tears, but this was just there.

So when we came to the meeting – and I think this explains where the myth came from – I presented what I'd been asked to do, which was a couple of alternatives for an EAR logo, and after a while I said, 'It seems to me that this sounds more like a mission to the deaf, and there might be another way to approach it.' I then produced the TEAR Fund logo. There were raised hairs on the backs of necks and they said, 'Yes.'

Design played an important role in establishing the new organisation's identity. Striking use of black and white graphics and large photos created impact, while attention-grabbing advertisements ensured that people noticed Tearfund and picked up its message.

To relieve suffering

The Evangelical Alliance Relief Fund exists to relieve suffering in the name of Christ, in obedience to His command, and taking into account spiritual needs as well as physical ones.

Evangelical Alliance Relief Fund leaflet, 1967

Tony Neeves, who became Tearfund's Communications Director in 1974, had a professional background as creative director in a London advertising agency:

> A lot of the publicity other Christian organisations were putting out in those days looked pretty Victorian really. It wasn't designed by professionals, so it looked badly put together. There was very little corporate feel to what others were doing, and it just didn't look exciting.
>
> But when young people looked at Tearfund material it looked contemporary and it grabbed their attention. It looked exciting, it read really well and it was in a different age-frame.
>
> Tearfund had a massive impact because suddenly here was an organisation placing a whole-page exciting black and white ad, or sometimes even a double-page – it was unheard of. It just took the Christian world by storm.

Allied with strong design were compelling words. George Hoffman was joined in 1970 by Bill Latham (later Deputy Director of Tearfund), who had a background in journalism. In Tearfund's magazine *Tear Times* they established a style that was simple, popular and

Cliff Richard, George Hoffman and Bill Latham were key figures in the public face of Tearfund in its early days. Cliff Richard's star status helped the new charity to make a big impact.

One of the earliest areas of involvement for Tearfund was medical and agricultural support for the Chaco region of Argentina and Paraguay. In 1973 this was the 'ambulance' – and medical help was ten hours' ride away.

unashamedly emotive. An article by George Hoffman on his visit to Bangladesh in 1972, for example, said:

> In the face of such human suffering and degradation you force your-self to put up some kind of protective mechanism and walk past the sea of faces that peer at you from all directions. But it's a thin veneer, and sometimes it cracks.
>
> He was about seven years old. He just kept looking at me pitifully, as he carried his little sister. She lolled limply on his shoulder as the perspiration trickled down both their faces whilst the sun beat down mer-cilessly upon them.
>
> Stoic-like I looked away, shook my head and walked past, once again maintaining the unwritten law 'never give to beggars or give cash relief to individuals'. But it was one of the hardest things I've done to brush away that sticky little hand that clutched desperately at my arm:

Seek justice, encourage the oppressed. Defend the cause of the father-less, plead the case of the widow. (Isaiah 1:17)

'I cried because I had no socks, until I saw the man who had no feet' – an old Arab proverb.

Tear Times, Spring 1971, reporting on Tearfund's relief work with refugees in Jordan

Not by bread alone

❝ After travelling across the Bengal plain to the border river, we returned to Calcutta physically and emotionally exhausted.

Turning to my Bible, I continued from where I left off the day before, in the fourteenth chapter of St Matthew's Gospel: 'When Jesus came ashore he saw a great crowd; his heart went out to them, and when he realised how hungry they were he turned to the disciples and said, "Give them something to eat yourselves."'

I realised afresh that the compassion of Christ and the command of Christ have not changed. His heart still goes out and His disciples must still obey His command to feed the hungry and care for the needy. And that is what TEAR Fund is all about.

But why another relief fund? What is TEAR Fund's reason for existence in view of the proliferation of relief agencies? Well, first of all, we take seriously the words of Jesus when he declared, 'Men cannot live by bread alone'. Besides providing material resources, ministering to man's physical needs, we see the responsibility of sharing the good news of Jesus Christ which alone can meet a man's spiritual needs.

Moreover, we abhor the false separation between the so-called 'spiritual gospel' – 'so-called' because I see no such distinction in the Bible. The early Christians were thrust out into the whole world to declare the whole gospel to the whole man. And authentic evangelicalism has always practised and proclaimed this Biblical truth.

In a sentence, TEAR Fund seeks to share 'the saving word' in the context of engaging in all forms of social work – be it medical, agricultural or first-aid relief.

This then is why TEAR Fund only – and always – works through evangelical agencies who share this emphasis – be they national churches in a developing country, or a missionary society that is serving there. ❞

From the Director's Report, George Hoffman, *Our first four years*, September 1972

and I can still see those two big eyes that pleaded more eloquently than words.

When I got back to where I was staying the mask slipped … I just put my head in my arms and wept – unashamedly.

Tearfund's fresh and challenging approach was beginning to catch people's attention: their hearts as well as their minds. Its public profile took another leap when it found a staunch supporter in the world of pop music: Cliff Richard. The singer had become a Christian through meeting Bill Latham, a teacher at his old school, and Bill had introduced him to Tearfund. In January 1969 Cliff did two special concerts at London's Albert Hall, plugged on BBC Radio 1, to

New kid

❝ These new young people at Tearfund had no mission experience, but I think that actually worked to their credit, because they would do things that others were inhibited about, that were a bit more adventurous. *Tear Times*, for example, was a great watershed – I mean suddenly we had a magazine that's suitable to go in the back of the *Times* newspaper rather than some scruffy little bit of printing.

But Tearfund turning up like this and coming out with great statements, telling missionary society leaders what to do, and their youth in itself, put off these leaders: who do they think they are?

Meanwhile, Tearfund was doing soundstrips and then of course videos, much more professionally than we were – we were still into taking hours to show boring slides.

Tearfund was touching parts of the Christian community that hadn't been touched before. ❞

David Applin, Ruanda Mission 1972-82, Tearfund 1982-92

raise money for a Land Rover for medical work in Argentina. The events created a surge of publicity and put Tearfund well and truly on the map.

This was the start of a long involvement with Tearfund: over the first fifteen years of its life Cliff's gospel concerts raised more than £300,000, and he continued to support the charity in the following decades. His visits to Tearfund-supported projects in poor communities overseas helped to stimulate concern – and had a deep personal effect on the star himself. In 1993, when Tearfund was marking its

They can't eat prayer

The Evangelical Alliance newsletter of Summer 1969 reproduced this photograph of a Vietnamese refugee boy under the heading, 'Let us not love in words or in speech but in deed and in truth. 1 John 3:18'. Beneath the photograph were the following words:

❝ 'I can't eat prayer' said the caption. And above it appeared the face of this little boy.

He soon became known in evangelical churches and groups all over the country through the first of TEAR Fund's information posters. This poster spelt out some of the needs in underdeveloped countries and the EA's strategic opportunities for meeting them. Little did we realise then the response there would be. In a word: overwhelming. ❞

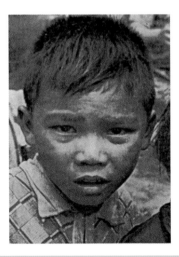

twenty-fifth anniversary, Cliff described a moment in a Bangladesh refugee camp in the early 1970s, when someone trod on a child's hand:

My instinct was to pick him up and hold him. In that instant, the smell and the dirt and the babies' sores didn't matter, and I learned a lesson that profoundly altered my perspective and understanding. A Third World image, previously sanitised and kept at bay within TV news bulletins, became reality; a statistic became a person. Through what was to be an appeal for funds, I personally encountered an appeal for love, and I realised I was in a position to offer both. By virtue of my public platform and so-called 'celebrity status', I had a unique opportunity to communicate what I saw and experienced and, via songs and video, was able to prompt others to pray and to give; by virtue of my Christian faith, I understood my obligation to reflect not my feeble sympathy but God's practical compassion.

> The righteous care about justice for the poor.
> (Proverbs 29:7)

Children are especially vulnerable in situations of poverty, and they have always been a particular focus of Tearfund's work.

The new charity also managed to spark controversy. In September 1968 Peter Meadows created its first poster for a mailing to churches, featuring a photograph of a Vietnamese refugee boy. What caused the storm was the slogan beneath it: 'I can't eat prayer'. It was deliberately provocative, to underline that Christian love has to be expressed in action, but for a Christian organisation with strong evangelical roots it was also risky. George Hoffman recalled later:

We thought an awful lot about it before committing ourselves, yet when one thinks again it is just what Isaiah was saying: 'What to me is the multitude of your sacrifices, says the Lord ... I have had enough of burnt offerings ... seek justice, correct oppression, defend the fatherless, plead for the widow...'

Tearfund's logo has
changed over the years:

The Evangelical Alliance Relief Fund

1968–86

CHRISTIAN CONCERN IN A WORLD OF NEED

1986–92

CHRISTIAN CONCERN IN A WORLD OF NEED

1993

CHRISTIAN CONCERN IN A WORLD OF NEED

1994–97

CHRISTIAN ACTION WITH THE WORLD'S POOR

1998–2007

2007–

The same concept, with a display of photos and the slogan 'They can't eat prayer', was used in the same month on an exhibition stand for Tearfund's first public appearance, the annual Christian conference at Filey, Yorkshire.

Perhaps inevitably, some who saw the slogan were offended. Peter Meadows recalled:

> We needed an advertising campaign, and that was the first line we ever wrote. It was a powerful line. But after only a few months one of George's assistants, an elderly, gracious man, said, 'You're going to have to withdraw the line and withdraw the advertising.' I said, 'Why?' and he replied, 'We've had a letter. There's a small group of elderly ladies who meet every week to pray, and what they're saying to us is, "You're telling us our prayer isn't worthwhile."' On that basis the line was pulled and never appeared again, until in 1973 it became the title of the first book written about Tearfund.

'They can't eat prayer' may have been too provocative for some, but it signalled that Tearfund was a young and radical organisation, intent on shaking up the church. While thoroughly Christian, and wholeheartedly evangelical in its theology and motivation, it was nevertheless willing to risk rattling the cage of the more conservative evangelicals and brave a degree of controversy in order to awaken the church to the Bible's strong call to active care for people in need.

The strength of Tearfund's initial impact was a matter of both style and substance. In its image and communications, the new organisation broke the mould. For evangelical Christians, it represented a bold and exciting approach that they were not accustomed to seeing from more traditional agencies. The substance was new too. Tearfund stated clearly and compellingly that there was a huge need in the world, and that the Bible demanded God's people do something about it. For Christians, here was a fresh and innovative channel through which they could express their concern for the needs of the poor. Tearfund offered them a rallying point and an opportunity for action, and they took it.

It was, in its way, a revolution.

Chapter 2

First Steps

Tearfund was all about putting Christian compassion into practical action, but important matters of principle were involved too. The reason? Tearfund came to birth at the centre of the one of the great theological debates of the twentieth century: the controversy over the 'social gospel'.

In earlier days, prominent Christian reformers such as William Wilberforce and Lord Shaftesbury had demonstrated that concern for poverty and social justice lay at the heart of the Christian calling, but by the end of the nineteenth century liberal theologians began to put forward a vision of the Kingdom of God which effectively

consisted in human reconstruction of society. To evangelical Christians, this was a betrayal of the gospel, reducing it to political action and social engineering – trying to build the Kingdom of God without God.

At the same time, the spread of pre-millennial teaching, with the implication that the world can only get worse until Jesus returns, turned many away from engagement with its needs. For some, it was

The plight of people struggling to feed their families struck a chord with evangelical Christians in the 1960s, resulting in an upsurge of giving.

This image from the 1975 Tearfund filmstrip *Walk in his shoes* challenged Christians to care for their neighbour's physical, as well as spiritual, needs.

even undesirable to try to reduce poverty and injustice in the world, because it might delay the Lord's return.

Many evangelical Christians and churches reacted against the 'social gospel' of the liberals by turning inward, spurning politics and other 'worldly' concerns and devoting themselves to prayer, Bible study, personal piety and 'saving souls'. The emphasis was on being saved out of the world as it headed for destruction, and helping others to find the same salvation. As Anglican minister and evangelist David Watson noted in an interview in 1982:

> Many of us such as myself grew up in a climate of polarisation between the so-called 'spiritual gospel' and the so-called 'social gospel'.

Tearfund was set up with a mission to take God's compassion to the world's poorest people in a way that met all their needs, material as well as spiritual.

Anything which smacked of the 'social gospel' was highly suspect and seen to be a dangerous diversion from the real work of winning men and women for Jesus Christ.

Glyn Macaulay, Tearfund's first chairman, recalled the state of opinion that prevailed in his own youth:

> **S**o you see, it isn't enough just to have faith. Faith that doesn't show itself by good deeds is no faith at all – it is dead and useless.
> (James 2:17, The Message)

There were a lot of people, and I certainly was included in their number in the early days, who were a bit baffled by the need for Christians to give to social needs. We had been brought up to believe that the Christian world is a tiny minority and our money and our resources ought to go towards evangelism, and that the rest of the world would look after the needs of the world.

Cop-out

❝ We have often talked and behaved as if we thought our only Christian responsibility towards non-Christian society was evangelism, the proclamation of the good news of salvation. In recent years, however, there have been welcome signs of change. We have become disillusioned with the 'cop-out' mentality, the tendency to opt out of social responsibility, the traditional fundamentalist obsession with 'micro-ethics' (smoking, drinking and dancing) and the corresponding neglect of 'macro-ethics' (the big issues of race, violence, poverty, pollution, justice and freedom). There has also been a growing recognition among us of the biblical foundations for Christian social action, both theological and ethical. ❞

John Stott, *Tear Times*, Spring 1983

10

TEAR FUND

THIRD W

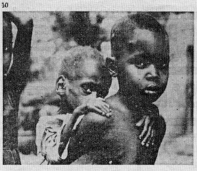

AFRICA: NIGERIA AND BIAFRA

Nigeria and Biafra is like a recurring nightmare that one is reminded of every so often by the odd TV news report or radio newscast. For the people who live and work there it's a daily reality: a living death. And there in the centre ministering to children and young people such as these, are Scripture Union staff workers Bill Roberts and Jane Sutton. Bill has been heading up the food distribution in Umuahia. Based in Ibadan, Western Nigeria, Jane, with the help of Tear Fund, has recently completed the first of a number of workcamps.

The Third World is the name given to the countries who are outside the Western nations and Communist block. In other words, they are the 80% of the world who exist on 20% of the world's wealth.

INDIA: MANMAD

Children, naturally enough, feature prominently in much of Tear Fund's ministry. So often in the Third World, they are the innocent victims; the rejects; the unwanteds. And the chance of their surviving to the age of four is ten times poorer than a child in the West.

Here are some of the more fortunate ones: they live in one of the Bible and Medical Missionary Fellowship orphanages in West India. Through the help of Tear Fund, essential improvements have been made to their home, which also houses refugees from Tibet. And in a letter just received from the superintendent expressing his thanks, he adds "I am glad to tell you nearly all of them came to know the Lord Jesus as Saviour: several old girls and boys are really active in His service."

JORDAN: AMMAN

This family were found huddled in a tiny, almost bare room, by Mr. and Mrs. Whitman, missionaries who are working with the Evangelical Free Church. They're there because floods swept away their little home and almost everything they possessed. Now, having been deserted by her husband and possessing no ration card, the mother copes as best she can.

Through Tear Fund aid they have now been given a new home, along with food and clothing.

AFRICA: BURUNDI

Sorry about the quality of the photograph. But you see, it's the light. A kerosene lamp is not the best light for photography ... nor for conducting major operations. But this is in fact the operating theatre of the Ruanda Missionary Society's hospital in Buhiga. And here the medical team of missionaries and national Christians work against impossible odds.

Yet less than a mile away is a series of waterfalls which if harnessed, could supply enough power to light a small town!

After a full survey and independent research, Tear Fund are embarking on their biggest project to date in harnessing this power and bringing light not only to this hospital but to the whole area, including the local school.

DEVASTATION

PERSIA: MASHAD

This kind of devastation can only be understood by those who have experienced it. In minutes, whole communities can be totally demolished by earthquake. Such was the case in Persia. Soon after the news came through, Tear Fund were able to go into action through the Worldwide Evangelisation Crusade whose missionaries in that country are based in Mashad, the very centre of the earthquake.

AFRICA: T

This is w like in par chance do have to gr little unless with them skill they And this Fund are p

A simple four-page insert in the *Church of England Newspaper* on 19 December 1969 outlined the vision of the new charity and showed it was already supporting work in a number of countries.

N THE RLD

This is the area of the world in which Tear Fund has been working during its first 12 months. Here is a selection of places where they are helping and the agencies through which they are working.

VIETNAM: DANANG

Surrounded by Viet-Cong near the town of Danang there is a remarkable husband and wife team. Their name? Dr. and Mrs. Stuart Harverson. Previously they worked with the old China Inland Mission; now they are serving under the Worldwide Evangelization Crusade in the heart of the war-zone area. There they have established an orphanage and give medical aid to many victims of the fighting

which is the constant background to all their work.

Here in the village of Ha Bac, Tear Fund has been able to supply villagers with rice, which is also administered by the Harversons.

One picks up something of the local situations by reports, such as the following: "Mortar shells still go off close by, and once I had to get on my cycle and hurry back to the orphanage, as I was in the line of a Communist offensive; but 'There are more with us than with them.' One evening we were closing the children's meeting with the hymn 'Jesus is mine—let nothing between'. As they dispersed one of them started singing 'I'd rather have Jesus than anything this world affords today', and they all took it up."

FREE CHINA: TAIWAN

Gladys Aylward, "The Small Woman", is back in China. News of her children's home in Taiwan reached Tear Fund when it was learnt that her 30 or so children had outgrown their old home and were in desperate need of new premises.

Tear Fund counted it a privilege, on behalf of Christians who had contributed, to cover the full cost of the move.

THAILAND: CHIENGMAI

Normally it is only the big wars, and fighting in strategic areas that makes the headlines. Meanwhile, throughout the Third World many live in fear of war and guerilla fighting. These are the prevailing conditions in North Thailand where Overseas Missionary Fellowship missionaries are working amongst the Meo tribe. Reports reaching Tear Fund stated that "just about all the Meo villages have been partially or totally burnt down, trails leading to villages are mined and have booby traps, some streams have been poisoned." Christians fleeing for their lives were machine-gunned from the air and "knelt on the trail in prayer whilst bullets flattened the area all around".

"Even as we write", said the missionaries, "news has just come through that another area has now been burnt and bombed. Blood and betrayals are now commonplace, and yet the other day when we left Lomsak we were deeply moved, as after the evening meeting the Meo crept under their mosquito nets and torches flashed on one after the other, as they had their individual devotions."

Another area in which Tear Fund has been privileged to channel "first-aid" help.

SOUTH AMERICA: THE CHACO

The Chaco, stretching across Paraguay and the Northern Argentine, is reckoned to have some of the most inhospitable conditions in the world. There the South American Missionary Society has been engaged in pioneer work among some of

the poorest people in South America. Here, this Mataco mother grinds her daily meal of beans. The staple diet.

And besides having the most inhospitable conditions, the Chaco also has the unhealthiest climate, and Dr. Michael Patterson, seen here with one of his patients, heads up the team of medical workers who have been battling against "killer" epidemics of polio, smallpox, measles, whooping cough and a tropical disease called trypanosmiasis.

Tear Fund are helping to assist them in this battle.

LATION

tian agriculturalist to work for four years in Morogoro, Tanzania, under the auspices of the Bible Churchmen's Missionary Society. There he will teach Africans to get the best results from their land by developing demonstration plots and advising the local farmers how best to raise their crops.

Evangelicals and global responsibility

At the October 1968 National Assembly of Evangelicals, Tearfund's George Hoffman presented a paper in the session entitled 'Our global responsibility'. He put five resolutions to the assembly, which were passed unanimously:

1. We confess that as evangelicals we have, to a large extent, failed to realise our social responsibilities and acknowledge our corporate involvement in meeting the physical, as well as the spiritual, needs of men.
2. We recognise afresh that man is an integrated being and we pledge ourselves to redress the imbalance in our total ministry to meet the social/physical needs of men, believing that compassionate service cannot be detached from the Gospel.
3. We reaffirm that our acknowledgement and understanding of God as Creator demands a continuing concern for such basic human rights as freedom, justice, and equality among men, as well as order and peace and a fair distribution of the resources of God's world.
4. In their support for churches and missions working in the underdeveloped countries, we urge that Christians in this country should have a greater participation in and identification with them as 'caring communities' through their medical, educational, agricultural and social programmes.
5. In the 'phasing out' of facilities and agencies provided by Christian missions, we urge that Christians should continue to involve themselves with the continuing social work of government agencies etc in the development of the emerging nations.

George Hoffman later recalled: 'I passed the Rubicon then, I think. None of us was sure that the idea of an evangelical relief fund was going to catch on, and I certainly never expected that speech to get the reception it did. Afterwards a great surge of interest – letters, telephone calls, enquiries – and gifts resulted.'

This mindset was to undergo a significant change in the 1960s. Thinking evangelicals, particularly in the younger generation, were increasingly stirred by the Bible's call to engagement with poverty and injustice. Leading the challenge was author and theologian John Stott, who in 1983 would become president of Tearfund. For Stott, the key understanding was that Jesus did not only preach: his words were always accompanied by deeds; his compassion could be seen as well as heard. Stott called evangelical Christians to break out of their closed world and emulate Jesus in this ministry to the whole person. In 1975 he wrote a booklet for Tearfund, *Walk in his shoes*:

Our evangelical neglect of social concern until recent years, and the whole argument about evangelism and social action, has been as unseemly as it has been unnecessary. Of course evangelical Christians have quite rightly rejected the so-called 'social gospel' (which replaces the good news of salvation with a message of social amelioration), but it is incredible that we should ever have set evangelistic and social work over against each other as alternatives. Both should be authentic expressions of neighbour-love. For who is my neighbour, whom I am to love? He is neither a bodyless soul, nor a soulless body, nor a private individual divorced from a social environment. God made man a physical, spiritual and social being. My neighbour is a body-soul-in-community. I cannot claim to love my neighbour if I'm really concerned for only one aspect of him, whether his soul or his body or his community.

A new sense of confidence emerged at the 1967 National Evangelical Anglican Congress, held at Keele University. For the first time, a national evangelical gathering in the UK gave support to the need for

Evangelical theologian and author John Stott taught the church that being a Christian was about action as well as words, and helped pave the way for Tearfund.

Active love

'By this we know love, that he laid down his life for us; and we ought to lay down our lives for the brethren. But if any one has the world's goods and sees his brother in need, yet closes his heart against him, how does God's love abide in him? Little children, let us not love in word or speech but in deed and in truth' (1 Jn. 3:16–18)…

We know what Jesus did. He saw, he felt, he acted. What about us? If we don't apply what we have to what we see, we are 'closing our hearts' against our needy brother. And if we do that, John is provoked to ask the angry question: 'how does God's love abide in us?' It doesn't. It cannot, for divine love is service, not sentiment. So if his love is truly within us, it is bound to break out in positive action, in relating what we have to what we see. No wonder John ends with an appeal to us to be sure our love expresses itself not 'in word or speech but in deed and in truth'.

John Stott, *Walk in his shoes*, 1975

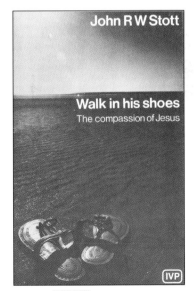

social involvement. Professor Norman Anderson, a leading evangelical, stressed that Christians must work not only for the redemption of individuals but also for the reformation of society, reminding them, 'We have tried to be the light of the world ... from a rather remote lighthouse.' The final statement drawn up by the congress said:

> We believe that our evangelical doctrines have important ethical implications. But we confess to our shame that we have not thought sufficiently deeply or radically about the problems of our society...
>
> God's purpose is to make men new through the gospel, and through their transformed lives to bring all aspects of human life under the Lordship of Christ. Christians share in God's work of mission by being present among non-Christians to live and to speak for Christ, and in His name to promote justice and meet human need in all its forms. Evangelism and compassionate service belong together in the mission of God.

> I know that the Lord secures justice for the poor and upholds the cause of the needy. (Psalm 140:12)

The following year, Tearfund's George Hoffman presented a paper on global responsibility at the National Assembly of Evangelicals in London, challenging those present with words from John Taylor's recently-published book *See for yourself*:

> The ambassador of Jesus Christ can never limit his efforts to only one aspect of need, whether spiritual or physical, social or individual. He knows that his Lord is the Saviour of the whole man and the whole of humanity, and he cannot rest content until all levels of experience and all dimensions of life have been rescued, healed, forgiven and made new.

It was time, he said, to stop perpetuating 'the myth of the false dichotomy – the social and the spiritual Gospel'. Evangelicals had the theology: the question was, did they have the compassion? The response of the conference

Point of view

" Do you realise if we start feeding hungry people things won't get worse, and if things don't get worse, Jesus won't come? "

Comment by a US Christian college student to Tom Sine, quoted in his book *The mustard seed conspiracy*, 1981

" Jesus of Nazareth was moved with compassion by the sight of needy human beings, whether sick or bereaved, hungry, harassed or helpless; should not his people's compassion be aroused by the same sights? "

John Stott, *Issues facing Christians today*, 1984

was unanimous. It adopted a resolution affirming that 'as evangelicals we have, to a large extent, failed to realise our social responsibilities and acknowledge our corporate involvement in meeting the physical, as well as the spiritual, needs of men'. Those present went on to 'recognise afresh that man is an integrated being' and pledged themselves 'to redress the imbalance in our total ministry to meet the social/physical needs of men, believing that compassionate service cannot be detached from the Gospel'.

This recognition was not confined to British shores. The central issue was a topic of debate in evangelical circles around the world – a debate that reached a turning point at one of the major world gatherings of Christian leaders in the twentieth century, the International Congress on World Evangelization, held at Lausanne, Switzerland, in 1974.

The Lausanne Covenant which resulted from the congress included a section entitled 'Christian social responsibility'. Here, the delegates expressed penitence for having viewed evangelism and social action as mutually exclusive concepts and affirmed the legitimate place of socio-political involvement in the Christian life:

> We affirm that God is both the Creator and the Judge of all men. We therefore should share His concern for justice and reconciliation throughout human society and for the liberation of men from every kind of oppression. Because mankind is made in the image of God, every person, regardless of race, religion, colour, culture, class, sex or

In 1974 the Lausanne Covenant affirmed that social and political involvement was a legitimate part of the Christian life. Tearfund showed evangelical Christians in the UK how to put their concern and compassion into practical action.

Malawi, 2002: An emergency food distribution near the border with Mozambique by Tearfund's partners Emmanuel International and the Evangelical Baptist Church of Malawi.

age, has an intrinsic dignity, because of which he should be respected and served, not exploited. Here too we express penitence both for our neglect and for having sometimes regarded evangelism and social concern as mutually exclusive.

Although reconciliation with man is not reconciliation with God, nor is social action evangelism, nor is political liberation salvation, nevertheless we affirm that evangelism and sociopolitical involvement are both part of our Christian duty. For both are necessary expressions of our doctrines of God and man, our love for our neighbour and our obedience to Jesus Christ. The message of salvation implies also a message of judgment upon every form of alienation, oppression and discrimination, and we should not be afraid to denounce evil and injustice wherever they exist. When people receive Christ they are born again into his kingdom and must seek not only to exhibit but also to spread its righteousness in the midst of an unrighteous world. The salvation we claim should be transforming us in the totality of our personal and social responsibilities. Faith without works is dead.

Tearfund came into being at a time when increasing numbers of evangelical Christians in the UK, especially the younger generation, were growing frustrated with the blinkered and narrow vision of the past. Against the backdrop of the 1960s, with radicalism, optimism and revolution in the air, young Christians showed an increasing desire to take their faith into society, to reject their forebears' isolation, to engage with a world that so badly needed change. Stephen Rand, who worked for Tearfund from 1979 to 2004, first as the coordinator of its volunteer network and later as Communications Director, was part of this generation of young people in the late 1960s:

> I was a student at that time and I was passionate about the need to do something about poverty. I was appalled by the church's complacency, and I suspect there were lots of people like me who were grateful to discover there were Christians trying to do something about it, people

Visible love

⟪ The Tear Fund story is not just one of growth. It is, I believe, an authentic expression of God's all embracing love for man – meeting him at his point of need. We see, and we serve, men not just as 'stomachless souls', needing to be saved. Or 'soulless stomachs' needing to be fed. But as men who need to be made whole. As John Stott argues in his book, 'Christian Mission in the Modern World', 'If we love our neighbour as God made him, we must inevitably be concerned for his total welfare, the good of his soul, his body and his community.'

And it's this distinguishing feature that I focus upon whenever I'm asked about Tear Fund's distinctive emphasis. In a sentence, if our love is to be credible, like God's love, it must be visible as well as audible! ⟫

George Hoffman, *Tear Times*, July 1978

who recognised that part of living responsibly in a modern world was doing your bit about poverty. And I think once they decided Tearfund was OK they stuck with it – it became part of their way of life. For some of these people it was a biblical conviction that this was something they must do, and John Stott was incredibly influential in this.

Tearfund started life as the Evangelical Alliance Relief Fund, and getting emergency relief to those who need it most has remained an important part of its work.

There was a hunger for a bigger vision, for a faith that could make a difference on the streets with the homeless, in the refugee camps with the hopeless, in every part of the world where people were suffering from poverty and injustice.

This was the wave of energy, passion and faith that Tearfund caught. In God's providence, it emerged just at the right time. To put it simply, it scratched where people in the evangelical world were itching: for people looking for a balanced faith, Tearfund provided an answer. As John Boxhall, a member of the original Tearfund committee and later its second chairman, put it in 2003,

Tearfund's supporters took the message of Christian social action onto the streets. Here, supporters in Cardiff in 1983 raised the profile of water needs in the developing world.

Tearfund was a product of timing as well as the right people at the right time. Reflecting over more than thirty years, to me it appears that God just brought the people, the time and the church together for a change.

For Dewi Hughes, who joined the staff of Tearfund in 1987 after several years as a volunteer and became its theological adviser in 1996, there was a similar sense that the early days of Tearfund represented a special moment in what God was doing with the church:

> I think that you've got to talk in terms of kairos moments and divine guidance – that God was doing something special here. I don't think there is any other explanation. I have a very strong conviction that Tearfund was a work of God and that it created a focus, a place that people can identify with.

For another of those involved in the early days of Tearfund, its emergence seemed to be part of what God was doing in awakening the church to a new

Gospel

❝ The Gospel is for the whole man, and is relevant to the purely temporal concerns of life as well as the most 'spiritual'. ❞

One world, one task, report of the Evangelical Alliance Commission on World Mission, 1971

Lopsided

❝ Evangelicals have beaten the living daylights out of the 'social gospel' during the past decade or so. What we have not done is to replace it with a biblical doctrine of social involvement. So that on the one hand we've got 'a Christian presence' in social involvement – which to me, on its own without the proclamation of the gospel, is meaningless. And, on the other, we have the proclamation of the gospel and no social involvement, which is lopsided! Evangelicals are so afraid of 'good works', as such, that in some cases this fear is excused as an excuse for not getting involved. But this lack of involvement is not theologically motivated – it is motivated by sheer indifference. And this indifference cannot be maintained much longer, when more and more opportunities for social involvement knock on their door asking 'Look! Here is need. What are you going to do?' ❞
Harry Sutton, General Secretary, South American Missionary Society, quoted in *They can't eat prayer*, Mary Endersbee, 1973

understanding of the world and the place of Christians in it. Tony Neeves later recalled:

The mood of the times was that we've got to reach out and win souls for Christ, and it seemed that was all the church was focused on – that and your own spiritual depth and growth. Yes, of course it was nice to do something for the poor people but it wasn't a biblical mandate.

It seemed to me at the time that the start of Tearfund was a watershed. The bulk of mission seemed to be dull – it just didn't seem to be very relevant to the younger generation. But George Hoffman had the ability to reach out to the younger mindset: you'd sit and listen to George and you couldn't help but be inspired and motivated. He was very much the spearhead of exposing the false dichotomy between the spiritual and physical aspects of human need. I think the church began waking up and realising.

From the very early days we believed it was very important to educate Christians, because we felt an educated donor becomes a committed donor. They're not giving purely out of an emotional response, although emotion does come into it, but giving because they have thought it through and are convinced this is the right thing to do.

We wanted to wake up the church to the issues of justice for the poor and the oppressed, because it's not just a question of pity, it's an issue of justice. We knew that we couldn't be incredibly deep initially, but we

Church

❝ The Early Church, in short, was a community in which compassion for those in either spiritual or material need was constantly being demonstrated and was a living part of her witness … The church, including the local congregation, should be seen to be involved in social concern as part of its total witness. ❞
One world, one task, **report of the Evangelical Alliance Commission on World Mission, 1971**

First grant

What exactly was the first grant Tearfund ever made? It's sometimes been said that it was the purchase of a Land Rover for use among the Chaco Indians of Argentina in November 1968. That's because it was the subject of 'Project Correspondence No 1', but that doesn't necessarily mean it was the first grant – it was just the first dealt with under a new system of numbering.

Grants were made throughout 1968, as the Evangelical Alliance Relief Fund Committee continued its work. It could have been the first grant made after the committee decided in July 1968 to adopt the name 'TEAR Fund'. But as far as the young organisation itself was concerned, it was a little later: according to *Tear Times* in Spring 1972, its 'first official project' was a grant of £250 towards flood relief in Argentina – in October 1968.

wanted to keep gnawing away long-term at this issue of it being the biblical mandate for social concern. That was what drove us.

We were trying to say that caring for poor and suffering people is part of Christian living. If you call yourself a Christian you cannot escape the fact that this is what God is calling us to do. It's a biblical command that we do this, and so it's a way of saying to Jesus, 'I respect what you say, I am not going to ignore what you say. You've said that we should do this and we want to do it because we want to please you.'

Early definition of Tearfund

❝ TEAR FUND exists to relieve suffering. It operates in the name of Christ, in obedience to His command, taking into account spiritual needs as well as physical ones. It encourages and enables Evangelical Christians in Britain to exercise a compassionate ministry for those in need both at home and abroad. ❞

From Tearfund's first policy statement, November 1968

To mark Tearfund's first anniversary, a special four-page broadsheet supplement was inserted in the 19 December 1969 editions of the *Church of England Newspaper* and the *Christian Record*. This was the first regular Tearfund publication, taking the middle four pages of the *Church of England Newspaper* once a quarter for the next four years. From the second issue, in early 1970, it was entitled *Tear Times*. The 1969 edition took the form of questions and answers about Tearfund by George Hoffman. Stressing that the Christian 'has a responsibility to preach... and to provide', he confirmed that Tearfund's aim was holistic: 'Working through evangelical churches, societies and other agencies abroad,' he wrote, 'we shall ensure that we are caring for "the whole man", spirit and soul as well as mind and body.'

This mandate, of course, had to be turned into decisions and

Opposite: Tearfund celebrated its first anniversary with a special report distributed with the *Church of England Newspaper* in December 1969.

CEN/RECORD DECEMBER 19, 1969

9

TEAR FUND

FIRST ANNIVERSARY

The Rev. George Hoffman, Organising Secretary of T e a r Fund answers some questions about the rise and growth of The Evangelical Alliance Relief Fund.

How did Tear Fund start?

Like Topsy—it just "growed". It grew out of a rising sense of concern for the plight of the third world and the gap that exists between "them" and "us".

And it grew out of a corporate desire to make it quite clear that Evangelicals do care about physical and material needs, along with spiritual ones.

Was there anything in particular that gave added impetus to the need for a special fund?

Yes. At the National Assembly of Evangelicals held in London at the end of 1968, the Conference unanimously confessed "that as evangelicals we have, to a large extent, failed to realise our social responsibilities and acknowledge our involvement in meeting the physical, as well as the spiritual needs of men".

And they went on to "recognise afresh that man is an integrated being" and pledged themselves "to redress the imbalance in our total ministry to meet the social/physical needs of men, believing that compassionate service cannot be detached from the Gospel".

So at least this was one conference resolution that didn't dissipate with hot air and post-conference euphoria?

Yes. The resolutions were laid firmly at the feet of the EA's social responsibility group who had been aware for some time of the desire and the need for a clearly defined and overt social action agency, that was unequivocally evangelical.

And now you've been going for 12 months. Are there any indications that your action in setting up a separate agency was justified?

Quite a few. For instance, there's the income of £40,000 which is a pretty phenomenal income for the first year of a new charitable organisation—particularly in the relief field.

There are files of "Thank-you" letters from people all over the world, including letters from a tiny Christian community in Peru whose homes were devastated by a hurricane; there are photos such as those of the children in Da Nang who are being cared for by Dr. and Mrs. Stuart Harverson with the aid of Tear Fund supplies; there's the encouragement of missionary secretaries at home, and Church leaders overseas . . . and, not least, there's the dozen or so requests for medical supplies, building materials, food and agricultural equipment on my desk at the moment.

No doubt you must receive queries regarding the necessity for yet another relief fund?

True enough. In reply we stress first the question of responsibility.

First there's our responsibility to our brethren in Christ in the developing countries who live in such appalling conditions with such desperate needs.

Secondly there's our responsibility to Evangelicals working in those conditions and in needy areas. We have a responsibility to help them to show people there that Christ loves them and that Christians care for them in their need. And this is particularly true in the case of natural disasters when overnight a whole community is wiped out. In the first 12 months alone, aid has been sent to the victims of floods, famines, a hurricane,

a typhoon, an earthquake and war.

Furthermore, with such ghastly situations in the third world, we believe we have an added responsibility—like the Catholic and Quaker agencies have to their constituencies—to arrest the attention of Evangelicals in this country, and inform them of the needs, requirements and the opportunities. And to ensure that the biblical balance in Christian ministry is maintained.

What do you mean by that last remark, "The biblical balance in Christian ministry?"

Quite simply, as Philip Crowe wrote in "Mission in the Modern World", "Service and evangelism are inseparably connected in the nature of man. Man cannot be divided into separate parts, and must not be treated as if he can. God has made man an integrated being. He is neither 'a soul with ears' nor 'a hungry man with no ears'."

In his closing remarks to the Christians at Thessalonica, Paul prays that God would "establish them in every good work and word". That's it in a nutshell.

In other words, as we have said in our advertising campaign, you cannot separate the social work from the saving word. The Christian has a responsibility to preach . . . and to provide.

Or again, to quote Mr. Crowe, "The evangelistic message must be linked to compassionate service just as a mission of compassionate service must include evangelism. The essential nature of man requires both".

And what about the other agencies? What reactions have you received from them as a newcomer in the field?

Nothing but encouragement and co-operation. Shortly after Tear Fund had been launched, the Rev. Alan Brash, the director of Christian Aid, invited me to see him, and we discussed together the distinctive role and contribution that Tear Fund could make in the developing world.

And Oxfam couldn't be more helpful. Besides being given a full tour of their headquarters and introduced to their executive officers, David Carter, assistant to the director of Oxfam, has advised us on numerous enquiries and put us in touch with the appropriate representative. Next year, following the suggestion of the East African secretary, Tear Fund and Oxfam plan to co-operate together in setting up a hydro-electric scheme in conjunction with the work of the Ruanda Missionary Society in Buhiga.

How many are there on the Tear Fund staff?

No one full-time! So far. My colleague, the Rev. Charles Phillimore, who deals with the office administration is, like myself, an Assistant Secretary of the Evangelical Alliance, which means that both of us have other responsibilities within our organisation. We have a tem-

porary education officer, Mr. John Pettingell, who plans to do post-graduate research work, and then there are our respective secretaries.

Well, how on earth do you operate?

At the risk of a gratis commercial for a well-known banking group — "our roots are our branches".

So far Tear Fund has been largely supported through personal members of the EA together with affiliated churches, groups, organisations and area fellowships. This of course has kept administration down to a minium as the machinery for channelling information and receiving support already exists within our main office.

Then over the last 12 months we've recognised the strategic value of working in the closest co-operation with the Evangelical Missionary Alliance — one of our associated departments in the EA. Consequently through these 90 affiliated missionary societies, including societies such as OMF, WEC, ECMS and SAMS, we have a world-wide network that is second to none.

And again, by operating through them and co-operating with them both in first-aid relief and in developing projects, the necessity for an additional administrative set-up has been avoided. Furthermore they are involved at ground level in the local situation—a most important factor in any relief programme.

And what about the additional responsibility you have personally taken on as consultant and co-ordinator of the International Christian Assistance Programme set up by the World Evangelical Fellow~~ship? How will this fit into~~ your work?

This new opportunity will of course be complementary to the work I am already doing. But more. At the risk of a mixed metaphor, it will be another world-wide "branch" with "roots" in every country. It will give greater contact with the national church and national Christians in the Third World as well as giving me a link with evangelical social action programmes and agencies throughout the rest of the world. And already this has happened with the support that has come in through the World Evangelical Fellowship for our relief programme in Tunis.

And what of the future? What are your plans for the next 12 months, say?

Well, first of all, to consolidate our world-wide network of communications and co-operation through the Evangelical Missionary Alliance and the World Evangelical Fellowship. This will increase our effective distribution of aid and maintain our economic administration which we believe to be important.

Secondly, with the tremendous interest and support which we have received from students and young people, we plan to develop this side of the work in particular.

Thirdly, we believe that it is of major importance to concentrate on development projects and "self help" training programmes in an attempt to utilise local resources and develop the area.

And allied with all the work abroad there is the basic requirement of educating and informing our constituency here at home of the facts and figures relating to the gulf between the "haves" and the "have nots". But, at the same time, working through evangelical churches, societies and other agencies abroad, we shall ensure that we are caring for "the whole man", spirit and soul, as well as mind and body.

'Removing the alibi'

The press coverage of Tearfund's launch event and first press conference in November 1968 reported Morgan Derham's comment that the creation of the new fund had 'removed an alibi'. This was a favourite saying of his: as he once observed, 'I've always had this thing about removing the evangelical alibi for giving to social need.'

He admitted that from the moment he was appointed to lead the Evangelical Alliance in 1966, he'd started work on this: 'I'd got a vision of what ought to be happening and what needed to be done, and part of that was that evangelicals should be getting stuck in to the whole business of relief and development and aid of that kind.'

Evangelical Christians, he argued, were holding back from too much involvement in overseas development, partly because the main church-related agency available at that time was Christian Aid and they weren't in sympathy with some of its theology and its links with the World Council of Churches. If this was a pretext for inaction, he argued, setting up a specifically evangelical channel for giving would remove the 'alibi' and evangelical churches would no longer have any excuse for sitting on the sidelines. Tearfund's creation meant the days of inaction were over.

actions, and for the new charity there were immediate questions concerning who should be given funding and who should not. Applications for support were coming in, and the committee knew it would need a consistent basis on which to respond. At its second meeting, in July 1968, it was divided over whether a request from a missionary in Uganda for help in rebuilding a school came within its remit. Did an educational project count as 'relief', or was it straightforward missionary work? Tearfund needed to maintain a distinction between its own vision for emergency relief and poverty alleviation and what it regarded as the traditional work and responsibility of missionary societies.

By November the committee had put together its first policy statement, which spelled out the criteria for funding:

Telling the world

" TEAR FUND exists to relieve suffering in the name of Christ. "

From the news release issued at Tearfund's press launch on 8 November 1968

Urgent requests for immediate help to relieve extreme suffering and famine will always be carefully considered and a large part of the funds available will no doubt be used for this purpose. Nevertheless it is hoped to control the proportion of TEAR FUND used for such 'first-aid' purposes in order to have available adequate sums for longer term economic 'pump-priming' projects such as agricultural education, well-digging, the construction of simple irrigation schemes, the provision of farm tools and seed and long term medical care projects. It is considered important not only to relieve

Tearfund posters in the early 1970s contrasted the comforts of western life with the poverty of the majority world.

Tearfund's press launch on 8 November 1968 juxtaposed silver candelabra with the meagre diet of 60 per cent of the world's population. The new charity's committee explained its aims (l-r: John Boxhall, Charles Phillimore, Peter Meadows, George Hoffman, Glyn Macaulay, Mary Jean Duffield).

immediate distress caused by natural disasters, wars etc., but also to seek to prevent the recurrence of such disasters.

It was also time to make a splash in the Christian media. Accordingly, the committee organised a press launch for 8 November 1968. The concept was original: the invited press found a table set for a grand dinner, complete with silver candelabra supplied by Mary Jean Duffield. The meal, however, was a surprise: nothing but puffed rice cereal, powdered milk and fruit. The point was simple but telling: as the handout explained, for 60 per cent of the world's population, a little rice was all they could expect to eat each day.

Covering the launch, *The Life of Faith* reported:

TEAR fund will channel gifts from Christians through Christians to all in need; so 'Evangelicals are now without excuse,' pointed out Pete Meadows. The Rev. A. Morgan Derham, Alliance general secretary, commented, 'The fund has removed an alibi.' No evangelical Christian can now shut his eyes to his responsibility to the world's hungry multitudes (60 per cent of the population in the developing countries suffer from malnutrition)…

Tearfund's income

In its first eighteen years Tearfund received a total of £50 million in donations. It took fifteen years to raise the first £25 million, and only two years and nine months to raise the second. By 2005, income was running at around £50 million in a single year.

Responsibility

❝ Why another separate Fund and Agency?

For the same reason that the Roman Catholics and Quakers have their own fund. It's a question of responsibility. First, we have a twofold responsibility to our fellow Evangelicals here at home. Our responsibility is to arrest their attention and to educate them about the needs. And then we have to ensure that their help is being used in the most effective and strategic manner through long-term projects as well as in 'first-aid' relief.

Secondly, we have a responsibility to Evangelicals working in underdeveloped countries and needy areas. We have to help them to show people there that Christ loves them and that Christians care for them in their need.

In other words, we want to take the Bible seriously when it says:

'If a brother or sister is ill-clad and in lack of daily food, and one of you says to them "Go in peace, be warmed and filled," without giving them the things needed for the body, what does it profit? So faith by itself, if it has not works, is dead.' (James 2:15–17) ❞

From the news release issued at Tearfund's press launch on 8 November 1968

Formed this year, TEAR fund has already sent £11,500 to needy areas – Biafra, Hong Kong, Northern Argentina, Haiti, Vietnam, Persia, India, Jordan, Philippines, Paraguay, Nigeria. It has a two-pronged out-reach: short term relief, eg., Persia, following the earthquake; longer term projects, eg., Northern Nigerian scheme for land development and agricultural training, with its headquarters at the Vom Christian Hospital (Sudan United Mission).

Grants made by Tearfund in its first four years shed light on the early focus of its work. In India, for example, it paid for improvements to an orphanage run by the Bible and Medical Missionary Fellowship. In Rwanda it gave £10,000 to fund a clinic run by the Ruanda Mission, where mothers were taught the principles of a balanced diet and their children

> I have come that they may have life, and have it to the full. (John 10:10)

were treated for malnutrition. In Afghanistan it provided £20,000 to medical personnel of the International Afghan Mission. In central Africa it gave £8,000 to help build and equip the 'Albarka', a floating operating theatre run by Dr David Carling of the Sudan United Mission and serving the areas bordering Lake Chad, where 100,000 people had no access to surgical facilities.

It wasn't long before the new fund's income began to rise. In its first full month of operation, June 1968, it received just £720 7s 7d, bringing its total available funds to £3,161. By August, its income for

Tearfund has been involved in Afghanistan since the early 1970s, supporting Christian partners providing hope through decades of turmoil, conflict and suffering.

the month had gone up to £2,640 9s 4d, and by the end of the first financial year in March 1969 it totalled £34,021. Some 80 per cent of the gifts were from individuals, with most of the remainder coming from churches and groups. The donations were of all sizes, ranging from an anonymous gift of £1,000 to five shillings (25p) sent in by a pensioner.

In December 1969 the committee discussed what its financial target for 1970 might be. For George Hoffman, the £40,000 received during the first twelve months with minimal promotion and advertising suggested there was no reason why income in the second year should not be in the region of £100,000. His colleague Charles Phillimore queried whether it would in fact expand to such a degree, bearing in mind the restricted constituency from which it derived its support. The more optimistic Hoffman, however, thought Tearfund would expand to an even greater degree than currently envisaged, particularly because of the growing concern within its constituency about some other agencies.

John Boxhall once admitted that while Morgan Derham and George Hoffman were the engine and dynamo of the committee, he had the reputation of being the brakes. On this point too he was one of the more cautious voices:

> We were discussing the next year's budget. I said, I propose that we use the figure of £85,000 as the limit and we should plan for that for the next few years. If we plan on £85,000 then we will know where we are going and George will be able to prepare a budget within that figure. Well, within a year I had a red face because we were a long way above £85,000.

Aim

The aim of the FUND is to help Christians meet the needs of those around them. This is what happened in Persia when we were able to send directly to missionaries of the World Evangelisation Crusade who were ministering to victims of the recent earthquake. Through the FUND, victims of the war in Biafra will be shown that Christians are both praying for them and caring for them through the help we've been able to send them. The same is true for flood victims in South America, refugees in Jordan, and the homeless in Hong Kong. On a long-term basis we are supporting projects such as the Faith and Farm training scheme in the Sudan, and agricultural apprenticeships in Jordan.

From the news release issued at Tearfund's press launch on 8 November 1968

Indeed they were. By September 1971 the income for one month was almost as much as the total for the whole of the first year, and in 1972 the annual income broke the £200,000 barrier.

With confidence, encouragement and support, the 'new kid' began to grow up, and gradually took on signs of maturity – by February 1969, for example, it had acquired its own bank account. Inevitably the time came for the youngster to fly the nest, and within two years of the committee's establishment Tearfund became a separate entity, no longer merely a fund of the Evangelical Alliance. In June 1970 Tearfund Limited was incorporated as a company, and in November of that year its memorandum and articles of association as a charity were incorporated. Tearfund was finally registered as a charity on 6 March 1973.

In 1971 Tearfund gave £8,000 towards the construction and equipping of 'Albarka', a floating operating theatre run by the Sudan United Mission and serving the area around Lake Chad in Africa. Its first patient was a Muslim imam who had suffered eighteen years of abdominal pain.

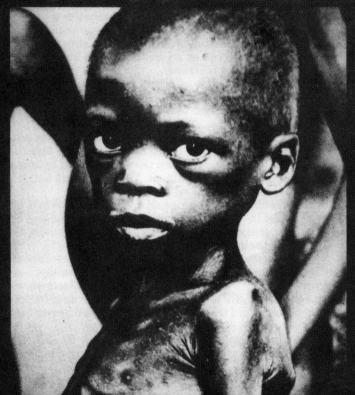

JOIN ME FOR LUNCH ON SUNDAY

I can't offer you much, but perhaps you won't mind going a little hungry for just one day.

Remember that two-thirds of the world's people always feel hungry – and 12,000 of us die of starvation each day.

If you will join me for a sparse meal, then April 29th – TEAR Fund Sunday – is the date to plan for. On that day

Christians will be getting together as families or in church fellowships to focus their prayers and attention on hungry and suffering people the world over.

TEAR Fund will use the money you save to bring help quickly and in the Name of Christ to those who need it most.

Please don't forget us.

TEAR FUND

19 Draycott Place, London SW3 2SJ

APRIL 29th IS TEAR FUND SUNDAY

First gifts

❝ Would you kindly send the enclosed five shillings to the hungry. I am crippled with arthritis and cannot go out, but thank God, at least I am not starving.
London W9

I would like the enclosed £12 to go towards feeding the hungry, please. This being the tithe of three old-age pensioners.
Edinburgh

I am so deeply moved by the Tear Fund poster you recently sent to me that I feel I must send a gift for this … unfortunately my gift cannot be large, but I send this gift of £1 with every good wish for the success of your wonderful work.
Westbrook, Kent

I have pleasure in enclosing a cheque for the sum of £80 to be used in the work of Tear Fund. This money was raised by holding an informal music evening, including a bring-and-buy stall and the sale of refreshments. The effort was organised by some of the young people of the Church of the Holy Trinity, Redhill, Surrey. With the cheque go our prayers that the work of relief through evangelicals may flourish.
Redhill, Surrey ❞

A selection of letters received in the early days of Tearfund

Opposite: Hard-hitting advertising for Tearfund Sunday, 1973.

When the donations came in pound notes… Tearfund's first administrator Charles Phillimore counts the income in 1970. In the year ending March 1970 Tearfund's income was £55,451.

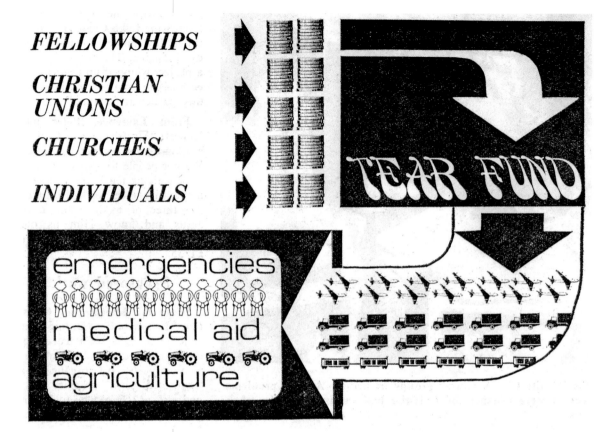

FELLOWSHIPS

CHRISTIAN UNIONS

CHURCHES

INDIVIDUALS

TEAR FUND

emergencies

medical aid

agriculture

In 1971 *Tear Times* showed in simple form how donations from Christians translated into practical aid around the world.

Requests for funding began to come in for projects in all parts of the world. By September 1971 the committee found that despite rapidly growing income, for the first time it had more projects on its agenda than funds available. In its publications, Tearfund urged supporters not just to give, but also to pray – not least that God would guide its leaders as they assessed the mounting requests being put to them.

Chapter 3

Emergency Aid

Sierra Leone, 2003: Ten years of civil conflict left nearly half a million people refugees. Tearfund's disaster response team provided clean water, sanitation and health education programmes. Tearfund's partner the Evangelical Fellowship of Sierra Leone distributed seeds and tools to families who had lost everything, and helped people come to terms with trauma.

'Tear Fund was born out of disaster' – so said *Tear Times* in 1981, as it reviewed the organisation's work in emergency relief. And indeed it was: responding to disasters was the original reason for its existence and has remained an important part of its work ever since.

Two major external events could be said to have helped trigger Tearfund. One was the crisis in the Indian state of Bihar, where famine had been declared on 20 April 1967, followed by catastrophic floods, which prompted an emergency call to the EA from Dr I. Ben

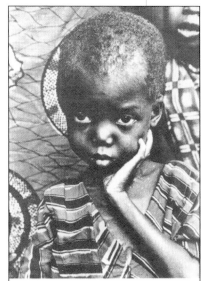

Thanks to
gifts from
crusade
readers and
many others

TEAR Fund, through
Bill Roberts (see p. 5)
is able to help
those suffering in
Biafra

TEAR Fund · 30 Bedford Place
London WC1

In May 1969 *Crusade* magazine carried this message. One of Tearfund's earliest ventures was to support Scripture Union worker Bill Roberts in his emergency relief work with victims of the war in Biafra.

Wati of the Evangelical Fellowship of India (EFI), asking for help. Christians in the third world were urgently appealing for help from their brothers and sisters in the UK.

The other was the war in Biafra, the eastern region of Nigeria which proclaimed itself an independent republic on 30 May 1967. The war lasted for three years, during which more than 1 million people died of malnutrition. For the first time television brought the day-to-day suffering of a war into living rooms in the UK. Technology was confronting UK Christians with the reality of humanitarian disaster, evoking a compassionate response from them.

The new relief fund emerged at what proved to be a historic turning point, where unprecedented public awareness combined with a clear opportunity to act. With both Bihar and Biafra, Tearfund was the bridge that enabled evangelicals in the UK to link up with a Christian response to disaster – emotionally and prayerfully, as well as financially.

Money was sent to EFI to support its famine relief work in Bihar, while in Biafra, Scripture Union worker Bill Roberts was resourced to help feed hungry people displaced by the war. As the months went by, Tearfund made grants to help relieve suffering in other disaster areas: to missionaries in Iran, where an earthquake had struck; to Argentina, where people had lost everything in floods, and to Haiti, where famine was so bad that it was reported mothers were selling their babies for two shillings (10p) rather than see them starve.

In 1970 Tearfund undertook its biggest relief effort yet, shipping out 100 tents, 5,000 blankets and 1,000 folding beds when prolonged rains caused devastating floods in Tunisia. Steve Levinson, a former missionary in Tunisia, was flown out to run the operation. As the appeal advert stressed, 'Once again Tear Fund's international network of evangelical contacts both here and, in this case, Tunis, enabled evangelicals to join with their brethren in need and help them to care in Christ's name.' The total cost of the programme was about £10,000.

The next major challenge arose in 1971, when East Pakistan

declared independence. The birth of the new nation of Bangladesh sparked a war, plunging millions of people into chaos. Just one year after 500,000 of its people had died in a cyclone and tidal wave, the country was the scene of an armed conflict which drove nearly 10 million to seek refuge in neighbouring India. With the defeat of West Pakistan's army, these civilians returned to find their country in ruins: an unparalleled disaster. The director of the UN's relief operation in Dacca said, 'There are no yardsticks to measure it. Previous relief operations around the world faced nothing so immense.'

Tearfund's response was launched when George Hoffman

An early disaster response operation: in 1970, emergency tents are loaded for shipment to Tunisia as part of Tearfund's response to devastating floods.

People under God

At the time of the genocide in Rwanda I watched the bodies just floating down the river. You stand there and you're thinking, what is it all about, what is happening? And yet then seeing people in those refugee camps actually trying to make it work, trying to make something better out of it, and the church getting involved – I remember just feeling actually it is amazing what people under God can achieve and do. That is a challenge for me all the time, all the time.

Jennie Collins, Tearfund 1992–2000

In 1971 Bangladesh's war of independence sparked a refugee crisis. Donations from Tearfund's supporters provided emergency help to 20,000 people.

returned from a visit to a teeming refugee camp in Calcutta, full of Bengalis who had had to flee their homes, leaving everything. While there, he had recorded his impressions on a dictation recorder, and on his return he played them to Peter Meadows and his music industry colleague Geoff Shearn. Peter Meadows recalled:

> In the background – I can still hear it now – there was the beeping of the lorry horns, and then you get George saying, 'Oh, the smell, oh no, she's holding my leg, she's holding my leg, she won't let me go, she wants me to take her baby. Ma'am, I can't take your baby,' and you could hear him crying. We listened to about twenty minutes of this and Geoff said, 'We need to get this recording into every church.' So he took it away, went into Pye Studios in Oxford Street and edited it down into a small version.
>
> We produced copies on flimsy little floppy vinyl 45 rpm records and sent one to every church on the EA list. No one had ever done it, not even secular organisations. Churches were just moved by it and began to play it. It was a kind of movement: that was the point, I think, where there was world need, and Tearfund was the bridge to deliver help from compassionate people. This recording said, 'Let's join it all up,' and that, I think, was a huge tipping point. It was the foot on the accelerator that lurched Tearfund forward.

Blaming God?

“ When people see a disaster on TV they often say, 'How could God possibly allow this?' Obviously it is true that God does allow it, but I have become increasingly aware of man's hand in disasters – the fact that disasters happen because of human actions and activities.

A war is an obvious example, of course. It's not God causing the war; it's one person pulling a trigger against another person. But even in natural disasters such as the 2005 Pakistan earthquake, it's absolutely clear that it's the poor people who get the worst of it every time. The rich people are in concrete houses with reinforced pillars, most of which stayed standing, whereas the poor people are in mud-built 'katcha' housing: they all collapsed, so it was the poor people who suffered. In famine situations too it's the poorer people who suffer most.

Time and again we see that it's all wrapped up in the social structures and mechanisms, and the extent to which resources are distributed equitably or not, and people help each other out or not. So even though people blame God for things like the 2004 tsunami, it's clear that if only we human beings got our act together and we all cared for each other and loved each other in the way we should do, many of these disasters would actually be a lot less significant in terms of human suffering. ”

Nigel Timmins, Tearfund 1996–

─ NURSES NEEDED ─

NEXT to the desperate need for shelter and protection, the most urgent need in Bangladesh is for medical personnel — especially nurses. It's hard to believe that in a country of 75 million squeezed into a land area the size of Scotland there are only 696 registered nurses.

In association with the Bible and Medical Missionary Fellowship, TEAR Fund are appealing for doctors and nurses who can go out for a short period to work in teams under BMMF supervision. Two areas of special need are the hospital in Dacca where many war victims require orthopaedic treatment and care, and at Mymensingh where the Australian Baptist Missionary hospital urgently needs help.

All enquiries to Mr. Arthur Pont, General Secretary, Bible and Medical Missionary Fellowship, 352 Kennington Road, London SE11, or to the Director, TEAR Fund, 19 Draycott Place, London SW3 2SJ.

In 1972 Tearfund's magazine *Tear Times* appealed for nurses to go to Bangladesh.

There was an immediate flood of donations, which enabled Tearfund to provide emergency help for 20,000 people. Among those Tearfund worked with in tackling the effects of the crisis was the relief committee of the Evangelical Fellowship of India, which had been one of the first relief agencies to go into Bangladesh. After initially providing temporary shelter and emergency supplies of food and clothing for the refugees, it embarked on building whole villages of small houses.

The Bangladesh crisis sparked another significant new development for Tearfund. In 1972 it appealed for nurses to go to Bangladesh for a short period and work under the supervision of the Bible and Medical Missionary Fellowship. This country of 75 million people had only 696 registered nurses, it said. More than thirty nurses and paramedical workers, together with seven doctors, responded. They went to Bangladesh for between six months and two years to work in feeding camps, clinics and hospitals.

One of these short-term volunteers was Jennie Collins, who spent a year in Bangladesh working as a physiotherapist:

I saw myself as being there to be involved with people who were poor and marginalised, who didn't have the opportunities that others had. I felt this was a valid thing to be doing. This was part of the gospel, part of what God wanted to happen in the world.

I worked in a hospital down in the south, and as a single woman I never went outside unless accompanied and having my head covered. I suppose I just began to feel something, perhaps, of what it might mean to feel oppressed and unequal. It was quite difficult. But on the other hand I felt how great it was that one could feel part of something bigger, part of the Body of Christ, the church of God which was bigger than just one place that I had experienced.

For Tearfund, Bangladesh was also a place for learning some important lessons about emergency relief. Jennie Evans joined Tearfund in

1973 as its Overseas Projects Administrator and served in many roles, including Director of Overseas Relief and Development. In 1974, she was asked to organise an airlift of emergency supplies to the new country, something she had never done before. Vaccines, drugs, vitamins, medical equipment and ten tons of powdered milk were obtained, five tons of blankets were purchased from Brentford Nylons and eventually a converted Britannia airliner was filled.

Nurses Rita Berry (left) and Liz Hutchinson (right) were among the dozens of medical personnel who responded to Tearfund's 1972 appeal for help in Bangladesh. Thirty-five years later, Rita Berry said, 'The situation there was desperate, and I felt God saying, "Come on, Rita: move!" So I went to Bangladesh for fourteen months. The experience changed me for the rest of my life.'

Inspiration

I shall never be the same again. I can't be. I have just seen how unequal our world is as well as witnessing the inspiring dedication of Christian missionaries and nurses doing all they can to help…

It seems to me that in this situation, humanity stops being human. People are too busy surviving to have time for love. Mothers are being forced to say, 'I cannot feed you, child.' And to simply watch them wither away.

These people are there at this moment and they *have* to be loved. I guess the only way we as Christians can love them from here is through our active support and by our prayers.

I shall be changed in that way certainly and changed in my attitude to people I don't know but who I know are suffering.

Cliff Richard, speaking after his visit to Bangladesh in 1973

Tearfund emergency relief supplies being unloaded in Bangladesh, 1974, overseen by Major Eva den Hartog of the Salvation Army.

Jennie flew out with the supplies to Bangladesh, then visited work in other parts of the country. Later she returned to the capital, Dhaka, where she was in for a shock:

> Someone took me around the market, and as I walked through it I saw Brentford Nylons blankets that had been cut into four and made into smaller blankets, and were being sold. I remember thinking, did I work my guts out just for these things to end up on market stalls? But then I realised that maybe that family's need for food was greater than their need for a blanket, and they'd decided they could maximise its usefulness by selling it and buying food.
>
> It was a very steep learning curve, and it was quite a turning point, I guess, in terms of the way we operated. It made us look at things more critically in terms of absolute need, to ensure that we weren't making available commodities or grants that we thought were needed but which actually were ineffective.

> **T**he poor and needy search for water, but there is none; their tongues are parched with thirst. But I the Lord will answer them; I, the God of Israel, will not forsake them. (Isaiah 41:17)

The ironic postscript to this story is that in September 1972, before Jennie joined the staff and unbeknown to her, the Tearfund committee had studied a *Daily Telegraph* report that 20,000 blankets sent to Bangladesh by Oxfam were being sold on the black market in Calcutta. A case, perhaps, of the painful consequences of not learning from others' mistakes.

Over the following two decades, Tearfund continued to send help to people suffering from disasters and emergencies, both natural and human-induced, in all parts of the world. Most often this was money to support the relief efforts of local Christian partner groups. For example, when famine hit Ethiopia in 1983, Tearfund enabled the Kale Heywet Church to purchase food for emergency distribution. In other cases it was personnel – as in 1979, for example, when Tearfund seconded medical and other specialists to Christian agencies working with Cambodian and Laotian refugees in camps in northern Thailand.

It was only later, however, that Tearfund began to function as an 'operational' agency, running its own programmes overseas. The first step towards this was taken in 1988, when it set up a dedicated post to manage its relief work. The job went to Mike Wall, who had previously worked in community development for Tearfund in southern Sudan. As Mike visited partner groups involved in disaster response,

Drought in Zambia in 2005 caused a catastrophic harvest failure. There was widespread hunger, but work by Tearfund's partner the Evangelical Fellowship of Zambia (EFZ) enabled some communities to withstand the disaster through improved farming and storage techniques. Stio Chizila (pictured) said, 'EFZ has shown us the way to go and is helping us to solve our own food problems.'

Disasters: the 'Crunch'

The Crunch model shows that a disaster happens only if a hazard meets a vulnerable situation. A hazard is an event that could lead to danger, loss or injury. One example is an earthquake. An earthquake in one part of the world can lead to the loss of many lives and the destruction of buildings, roads and bridges. However, an earthquake of the same strength in another country may cause much less devastation. This may be because buildings are stronger, communities are better trained or few people live there. A hazard by itself is therefore not a disaster. Only when the hazard meets a vulnerable situation does a disaster happen.

People are vulnerable when they are unable to adequately anticipate, withstand and recover from hazards. Poverty contributes to vulnerability. That is why an earthquake may cause a disaster in a poor country, while an earthquake in a richer country may have little impact. At local level, a hazard can cause disaster for poor households, while richer households may not be affected to the same extent.

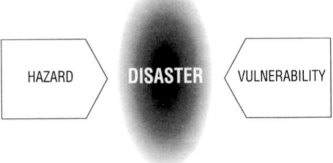

From *ROOTS 9: Reducing risk of disaster in our communities*, Tearfund, 2006

two points emerged: sometimes the groups trying to help were affected by the emergency themselves and so lost their ability to intervene, while in other cases, particularly in major disasters that needed a rapid, large-scale response, the local church simply did not have the capacity to respond.

It became clear that Tearfund should start developing its own capacity to provide direct operational assistance in an emergency, and in the early 1990s it started preparing for this, eventually setting up its own Disaster Response Unit in 1994. Mike Wall saw the hand of God at work:

> We did all the groundwork, creating a designated relief unit with a strategy to be operational – just six months before probably one of the most horrendous emergencies of the last twenty-five years: Rwanda. Suddenly this operational relief had to grow to enormous proportions, and I think God had prepared us for that.

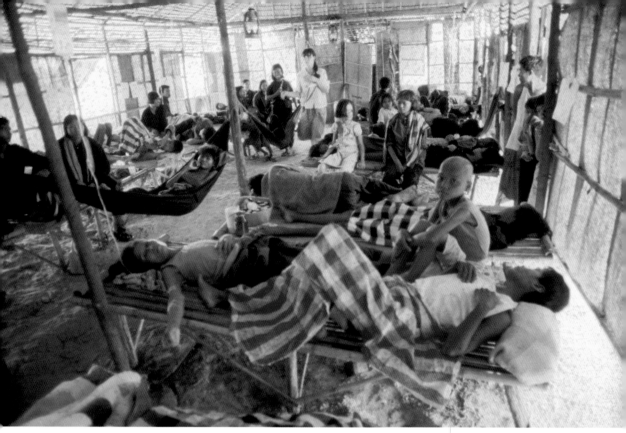

The outbreak of genocide in Rwanda in 1994 claimed 800,000 lives. Tens of thousands of refugees fled into neighbouring Tanzania and Zaire. The scale of the problem was far beyond the capacity of the church to help, and so for the first time Tearfund engaged in a large-scale direct operation, sending its own teams of workers to assist the refugees. A key factor in the success of this work was that it was undertaken in partnership with Christian Outreach, a more experienced operational agency from which Tearfund was able to learn a lot.

A camp clinic for Cambodian refugees in Thailand, 1979. Tearfund recruited medical staff to work with missionary societies in the refugee camps.

Tearfund personnel worked in camps in Zaire and Tanzania, providing community, educational and other support to the refugees. For Tearfund, it was not just a major operation, but also brought significant challenge and change, as Mike Wall recalled:

> **A**rise, Lord! Lift up your hand, O God. Do not forget the helpless. (Psalm 10:12)

It had always been said that Tearfund was the best kept secret: even in the UK most people had never heard of Tearfund. We were an unknown entity with the United Nations High Commissioner for Refugees (UNHCR), and we learnt that if we were going to be operational we needed to have a reputation – and a good reputation. The other thing Tearfund learnt was being professional,

Genocide in Rwanda in 1994 claimed some 800,000 lives and sparked a refugee crisis. The clothes of victims are displayed as a reminder at the Murambi memorial centre.

and really high standards were set. We weren't just going in and doing our own thing; we were doing it under the UNHCR and we had to meet the standards of good practice.

Since that start, Tearfund's operational capacity has steadily grown: by 2006–2007, Tearfund teams were working in Burundi, the Democratic Republic of Congo, southern Sudan, Afghanistan, Liberia, the Darfur region of Sudan, Indonesia, Pakistan and Kenya, caring for people and communities affected by conflict and natural disasters.

The work with partners continued, however. While Tearfund personnel were working with Rwanda's refugees, in West Africa another

Message

A refugee camp is a soul-destroying place. People are displaced, disorientated, embittered and struggling to have their daily needs met. We provide opportunities for productive work which relieves tensions and rebuilds self-worth. Our goal is to live out the Christian message of love and reconciliation through our actions in the camps.

Paul Stephenson, Community Service Co-ordinator, Musuhura Hill camp, Tanzania, 1995

Rwandans who had fled conflict in their own country to neighbouring Zaire in 1994 improvised basic services in refugee camps. Tearfund mounted its first large-scale direct operation, in an alliance with Christian Outreach.

Resurrection

I was in Nicaragua three months after Hurricane Mitch, standing in a place where half a mountain had fallen off in a mud slide. It was just quiet. There was nothing but mud, and in the middle of it a couple of pieces of kids' clothing and some ashes where they had burnt the bodies, and a cross. Then I heard of a woman health worker who was the first person to get there. She had walked for twenty-four hours and spent two weeks working night and day just trying to help people. She was from the local church.

I think that is the world we live in; that's what it is like – the devastation and the hurt and the cross and the resurrection. That for me was such a moving experience: meeting absolutely ordinary people who do extraordinary things in the most far from normal circumstances.

Jennie Collins, Tearfund 1992–2000

refugee crisis was under way – in Sierra Leone, where rebels were waging a cruel campaign against the civilian population. Here, as Mike Wall explains, Tearfund worked with the Evangelical Fellowship of Sierra Leone (EFSL):

> We could have just turned up in Freetown, gone to the UN, been allocated a site and set up our own camp. But the work wouldn't have been so effective because we wouldn't have had the local contact. We set up a refugee camp with EFSL, however: it was EFSL's camp, and what we were doing was increasing their capacity. It also meant there was more Christian impact, because by supporting the work of an established local Christian partner we were strengthening their witness.

Tearfund's partners faced a huge challenge in October 1998, when the western hemisphere's deadliest hurricane in two centuries hit Central America, bringing devastating floods and mudslides. An estimated 10,000 people were killed. Gordon Davies was head of Tearfund's Latin America team at the time:

> The big thing was that our partners were already there and we were able to respond straightaway to some of them. Also, just eighteen months before the hurricane we had run a disaster preparedness workshop in the region: one Nicaraguan partner said to me afterwards, 'All I did was take my notes off the shelf and start using them.'

Existing partners had to scale up, and new partners had to be found, but the local churches and Christian organisations had the capacity

to cope. Tearfund supporters gave £2.75 million, which made it possible not just to meet immediate emergency needs but also to help affected communities rebuild their lives over the following four years.

The involvement of the local church was vital, because of its close relationship with the communities affected by the hurricane and its understanding of local needs. The fruit of the relationship was lasting, Gordon recalled:

> What we ended up with was a very strong network of partners able to deal with emergencies in the region: where there has been damage from smaller hurricanes since, they have been able to click straight in and respond. It was gratifying to go back later to visit some of the rebuilt areas and find a real sense of community, and exciting also to see groups of new believers meeting as branches of a church that had helped to rebuild homes.

In the same year as Hurricane Mitch – 1998 – Tearfund also launched a major relief programme in southern Sudan, where famine and the dislocation of war

Honduras, 1998: Hurricane Mitch killed thousands of people and destroyed homes and livelihoods here and in neighbouring countries.

Provided

God always seemed to provide us with the relief workers we needed, usually at the last minute. Tearfund never compromised its standards, and I think there was a sense of 'Those who honour me I will honour' (1 Samuel 2:30).

Steve Penny, Tearfund 1997–2001

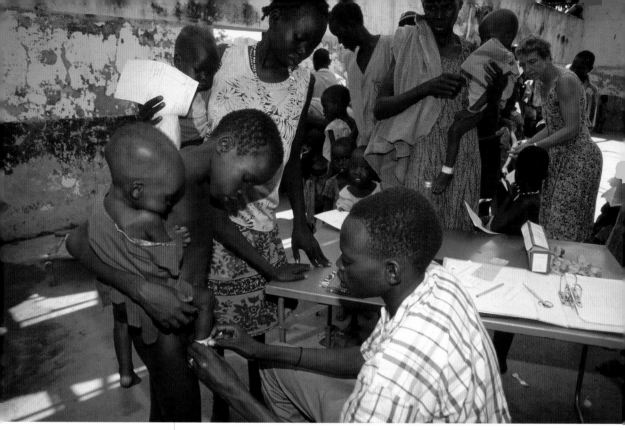

Sudan, 1998: As war and famine ravaged southern Sudan, Tearfund provided emergency feeding programmes for malnourished women and children.

had pushed the population into famine. At home, Tearfund joined the Disasters Emergency Committee, the umbrella organisation representing leading UK aid agencies. From now on, Tearfund's name would be one of those featured in national television appeals at times of major international disaster, and the organisation would also receive a share of the funds raised.

The famine in Sudan was followed in 1999 by conflict in the Balkans which saw thousands flee from Kosovo into Albania in Europe's biggest refugee crisis since the Second World War. Tearfund, already stretched, launched its fourth emergency appeal in twelve months. Steve Penny had been leader of Tearfund's Disaster Response Team since 1997:

The scale and number of disasters was putting the team under great strain and it led to a major rethink. It was decided to increase the size of the team and to redefine the strategy. We had been dealing

Seeing clearly

"" When you talk to non-Christian friends here after a disaster overseas they'll say, 'Well, I can't believe in a God who allows this to happen.' But if you go out and meet the people affected by the disaster, you find they actually cling on to God and see him a lot more clearly than we do – rather than blaming God they turn to him for assistance. ""
Nigel Timmins, Tearfund 1996–

only with conflict emergencies but now we widened our brief to deal with natural disasters too. We'd also been developing a lot of expertise in disaster preparedness and mitigation – helping vulnerable communities to be better prepared for disaster and to reduce their impact.

So the team became much bigger, not just to increase our operational capacity but also so we could provide more help to Tearfund's partners in their own response to emergencies.

Biafra

Any day now I shall be fully involved in relief work, using quite a number of SU members I hope. I am almost certain that it will be possible to translate the Refugee money which I brought out into Biafran cash for buying food and any other necessary things. It is the villagers who are now even worse off than the refugee camps because the latter have been receiving regular protein food for many months. We are setting up feeding centres where food (stock fish and milk etc.) is cooked and given out to the children mainly in the villages round about... We have been bombed nearly every day...

Extract from a letter from Scripture Union (SU) staff worker Bill Roberts to Tearfund, 11 October 1968, on his return to Biafra

For example, in January 2001, when the Bhuj earthquake hit Gujarat, one of the deadliest earthquakes in India's history, we didn't go operational but provided our partners there with the advice and support they needed to do it themselves.

Since then, Tearfund's ability to respond directly to disasters has grown considerably. Nevertheless, while developing its own operational capacity, Tearfund has continued to support the relief work of the local church around the world. In 2006–2007 it provided more than £9 million to partner groups working in emergencies.

Helping communities to prepare for disasters before they happen has a long history in Tearfund. As early as 1968, while the

The 1999 refugee crisis in former Yugoslavia, when thousands fled from Kosovo into Albania, led to an expansion of Tearfund's disaster response capability.

In the early 1980s nearly a million people died from famine in Ethiopia. Twenty years later, with many poor communities still vulnerable to the risk of food shortages, Tearfund's local Christian partners were working with them, helping them to build their capacity to deal with disaster. Here terraces to conserve soil and moisture are being built as part of a food-for-work programme.

committee was making its grants for emergency relief it was also asking if anything could be found out about schemes for preventative action. Answers, however, were not immediately forthcoming.

The first insights came from Ian Davis, a lecturer in architecture who started helping Tearfund with its audio-visual resources in 1970 but switched his interest to disaster management after a visit to Nicaragua in the aftermath of its 1972 earthquake. Ian became an internationally respected expert on disaster management and remained a consultant to Tearfund for more than thirty years.

In the late 1980s he and Mike Wall launched a programme of training workshops with Tearfund partners on disaster management, and in 1992 they produced a training manual, *Christian perspectives on disaster management*, which used appropriate Bible stories as case studies. A model of disaster management was developed, based on the concept of the 'crunch': that disaster occurs when a hazard such as an earthquake or flood meets a vulnerable situation – which is why poor people usually suffer most in disasters.

The concept of working to reduce vulnerability became increasingly important in Tearfund's work, as Ian Davis later explained:

Darfur, 2004: A million people were reported displaced by a campaign of terror and violence. Tearfund emergency response personnel worked in camps within the region, while its church partner in Chad cared for refugees who had crossed the border.

Tearfund started out as a relief organisation, which at that time meant giving disaster relief to people to get them back on their feet, and we saw that as a Good Samaritan role. There's nothing wrong with that, but it rather ignored the long-term issues of vulnerability and dealing with risk, and perhaps dealing with longer-term recovery. Over a number of years Tearfund started to shift gear and think much more about preventative action: helping people to prepare for disaster and to reduce risks.

Bill Crooks, who joined Tearfund in 1993 as Training Manager, continued Mike Wall's work in running training workshops in various parts of the world with Ian Davis, bringing together delegates from different countries and agencies:

We teamed up with Oxfam and other agencies, so it was a collaborative thing, and we had lots of Muslims come to our training and our Bible studies. It was quite groundbreaking in that it was the first time we did training with other agencies. At that time disaster preparedness was only being discussed at a fairly low level in the aid sector, and Tearfund was one of the few to start doing it.

Be prepared

In 1968 Tearfund, a little known and tiny organisation taking its first steps, provided modest sums of money for emergency relief in the Indian state of Bihar, which had suffered famine and catastrophic floods.

An indication of how far things have come since then is that in January 2005 the work of one of Tearfund's partners in helping communities in Bihar to prepare for and withstand disaster was featured at the World Conference on Disaster Reduction in Kobe, Japan.

Tearfund and the Indian Christian organisation Discipleship Centre (DC) reported on how DC had helped vulnerable groups to implement low-cost measures so that they would be better prepared for floods. These included building escape routes and raised hand-pumps, providing boats, and also setting up women's self-help groups, village development committees and flood response teams.

When severe floods came in July 2004, the measures spoke for themselves: the impact on communities where DC had been working was less than in neighbouring areas where it had not. DC's work was effective in saving lives, livelihoods and belongings. It showed the benefits of integrating disaster risk reduction with development – and highlighted the need for government to replicate this experience over wider areas. It was also economically effective: a study showed that for every one rupee spent on disaster risk reduction, nearly four were gained in quantifiable benefits.

For Marcus Oxley, who became Tearfund's Disaster Management Director in 2001, putting this approach into action became a top priority:

> Our approach is very much about helping communities to be better prepared, so that they're better able to respond to the impact of a disaster, but also about trying to prevent it occurring in the first place. That means looking at the factors that cause disaster and doing something to address them. This preventative work is called disaster risk reduction, and we think it should be built in to all development work.

In 2001 Tearfund started lobbying the UK government to put more emphasis in its own emergency aid policy on helping vulnerable communities to reduce the risk of disasters. Its 2005 report *Learn the Lessons* called for aid spending to shift from 'bandaging wounds' to 'preventing injuries'. It is testimony to the professional excellence achieved by Tearfund that not only did the government's Department for International Development incorporate this into its policy, but when it launched the policy in March 2006 it chose to do so at Tearfund's headquarters.

Tearfund's partners work with communities to help them prepare for disasters. Here, in Bihar state, India, villagers practise flood evacuation in boats they bought with help from Tearfund's partner Discipleship Centre. 'We used to dread the monsoons,' said villager Heeran Paswan. 'We did not know if we would survive. Now we feel at peace, because we know we can save ourselves.'

Building raised platforms for water pumps in flood-prone areas protects the water supply from contamination: an example of preventative action to minimise the damage done by disaster.

Forty years of involvement in disaster management have seen Tearfund grow out of all recognition in the scope, scale and professionalism of its work. From disbursing small grants of money to missionaries it has become one of the UK's top ten emergency relief agencies, respected for its good practice. Ian Davis witnessed the growth and development of its disaster response work from the very beginning:

In the early days Tearfund didn't have the confidence to engage with governments or UN people. But what a different atmosphere there is today. Lots of people are coming to Tearfund's doors now, and the salt is really getting out of the bottle, which is really encouraging. Tearfund is making a decisive global contribution in many areas. I was recently at a meeting in Montreal where the director of a UN agency put up on the screen that there were three

During this time some prophets came down from Jerusalem to Antioch. One of them, named Agabus, stood up and through the Spirit predicted that a severe famine would spread over the entire Roman world. (This happened during the reign of Claudius.) The disciples, as each one was able, decided to provide help for the believers living in Judea. This they did, sending their gift to the elders by Barnabas and Saul. (Acts 11:27–30)

After the devastating South Asian tsunami of December 2004, Tearfund and its partners helped 700,000 people in Sri Lanka, Indonesia, India, Thailand and Somalia. The initial response of emergency food and shelter provision was followed by longer-term work to rebuild homes, jobs and communities.

decisive organisations helping in disaster risk reduction: the Red Cross, ActionAid and Tearfund. I found that very encouraging.

Nigel Timmins, who joined Tearfund in 1996, worked on Tearfund disaster management programmes in many parts of the world and saw the change in its standing in the field:

> When I first joined, if you went overseas and said, 'I work for Tearfund' at an NGO forum they would say, 'Tear who?'
>
>   That doesn't happen now. You pitch up somewhere in the latest major crisis and say, 'Tearfund', and they say, 'Right, yes, what are you

Guatemala 1976: Children queue for emergency food relief after the major earthquake that struck at 3am on 4 February 1976, killing more than 25,000 people and injuring some 75,000 others. A letter to Tearfund supporters raised £75,000 – at that point the largest single response in the history of Tearfund. This funded distributions of emergency supplies and longer-term rehabilitation work by the network of forty local evangelical committees in the disaster zone, including rebuilding houses. Tearfund's consultant Ian Davis reported that many people had died when heavy roof tiles fell on them as adobe mud walls collapsed: he advised safer construction methods for the new housing.

Soft help

We're very good at providing the wells, the pots, the blankets, the 'hardware', as we call it, but actually the 'softer' side of things is equally important, particularly when people are going through a very traumatic time. These are the times when people need to feel they are cared for, they're loved, that somebody has empathy and is grieving with them. And these are the things that Christians and church-based partners and locals are particularly able to give, that secular organisations sometimes struggle to give.
Marcus Oxley, Tearfund 2001–

Zimbabwe, 2007: When thousands of people were suffering from water shortages, Tearfund helped its partner Churches in Bulawayo to set up water distribution points in the poorest areas.

Afghanistan, 2001: Tearfund launched an emergency appeal when millions of Afghans were threatened by food and water shortages after three years of drought and crop failure. Families were moving in search of food, and in Herat some 250,000 people sought refuge in a camp. Tearfund's partners worked in camps inside Afghanistan and in neighbouring Pakistan, providing food, water, shelter and sanitation.

going to do?' You are expected, and respected. Tearfund has grown in professionalism, and that is very valuable in terms of our witness to other agencies and colleagues.

The heartbeat of Christian compassion has not changed, however. In a world where the number of disasters is increasing, Tearfund's vision is to show the love of Christ in tangible ways to people who have lost everything. As Marcus Oxley explains, this work is a vital part of the witness of the church:

Values

❝ We did an exercise with the Disasters Emergency Committee, looking at the values of all the member agencies. The facilitator who came to Tearfund, a respected academic in humanitarian policy, said he'd never met an organisation where people's individual personal values, as evangelical Christians, matched the corporate values so clearly. He was bowled over by that. ❞

Steve Penny, Tearfund 1997–2001

As these crises increase, I think that our prophetic voice, our biblical message, will become stronger. We want to ensure that the church is prepared and better positioned to proclaim that message and to demonstrate it.

We can offer hope of a real salvation, and a better alternative. The church can demonstrate practically what that alternative is, what a transformed community is. At times of disaster the church has an opportunity to be at the fore-front, and to demonstrate the Kingdom of God.

Chapter 4

Creating Partnership

As the noisy infant Tearfund began to make its presence felt, there was some caution, even anxiety, among some of the long-established missionary societies. Was the new arrival getting too much attention? Was it in fact drawing support away from more traditional missionary endeavour? There was plenty of potential for tension. Ian Prior, who joined Tearfund as Overseas Personnel Secretary in 1973, later recalled:

> We were dealing with emergencies, which easily catch people's emotions and prompt them to give money. I think there was a fear in some of the missionary societies that we were capturing the money that they felt they ought to be receiving and using for longer-term work. People were highly motivated by disaster scenes and would offer for service overseas, when maybe they needed to be challenged by the long-term

What is Tear Fund?

❝ Tear Fund believes that 'man cannot live by bread alone.' For, in the words of Jesus, 'life is more than food and the body more than clothing.'

As the New Testament teaches, true meaning in life and fulfilment for life can only be found through a faith and trust in Jesus Christ.

Tear Fund therefore works in partnership with fellow Christians who share this conviction and who acknowledge that the Bible, as the authoritative Word of God, is the guiding rule of all Christian belief and behaviour. The supervision of any Tear Fund supported project is therefore always in the hands of those who want to introduce the people they serve to that 'fullness of life' which comes through faith in Jesus Christ alone.

And through its varied ministries, Tear Fund seeks to express this faith by practical service and evangelism, endeavouring to meet the needs of all members of a community, irrespective of their philosophy or ideology. ❞

Description of Tearfund and its vision used until 1987

needs a little bit more. So they felt we were cornering the money market and the people market.

In November 1969 Tearfund tried to allay these fears by holding a special consultation with representatives of a number of missionary societies. The man sent to speak in Tearfund's defence was Ernest Oliver, who played a key role in building its relationship with the societies. A veteran missionary leader, he became General Secretary of the Evangelical Missionary Alliance (EMA) in 1966 after long service in India and Nepal. John Boxhall's recollection of Tearfund's early decision-making shows that the range of his experience and contacts in the missionary world was of great help:

> No grant was made without the approval of the committee. George Hoffman used to come with lists of projects and proposals and recommendations, and would often rely very heavily on Ernest Oliver, saying, 'But do you know Charlie in India?' or 'Do you know Mary in Nigeria?' And Ernest would invariably say, 'Well, of course I do.'

The network of personal contacts was essential for Tearfund's early work. Apart from anything else, for a small committee in London with little means of monitoring the use of its funds overseas, it provided a helpful safeguard. As Morgan Derham noted at the time, 'You have evangelicals on the spot overseas, missionaries whom you know you can rely on to watch what happens to the money we send.'

The EA Relief Fund was clear from the beginning about who it wanted to work with. As early as 1968 it declared, 'The Fund exists for supporting both missionaries and national Christians who are fighting against hunger, poverty, ignorance and disease.' In practice, however, national Christians were in the minority, as virtually the only overseas contacts the fund had were missionaries and missionary societies.

Partnership

If you want to go fast, then go alone. If you want to go far, then you must go together.
African proverb

Opposite: In the village of Uhambingeto, Tanzania, Tearfund's long-standing support for the Diocese of Ruaha has brought many changes, including a fresh water supply, a dispensary, an integrated health programme teaching nutrition, and credit schemes enabling people to set up small businesses. As a result of this development, the government decided to build a secondary school there.

Understanding

When I am with Tearfund I know I am speaking to brothers and sisters who understand the mission of the church and subscribe to it totally; and that's exciting, very exciting.
Francis Mkandawire, General Secretary, Evangelical Association of Malawi

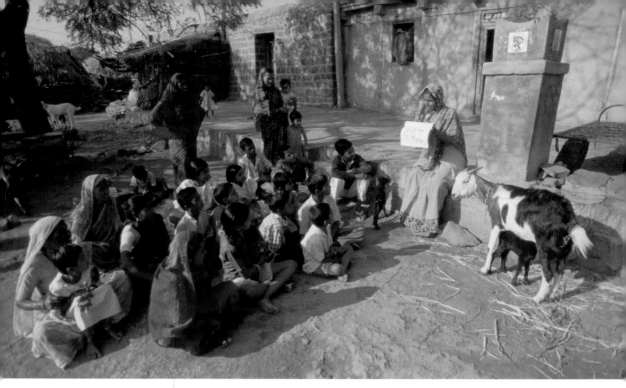

Sukhubai is a village health education worker with Tearfund partner the Comprehensive Rural Health Project (CRHP), founded in India in 1970 by Christian doctors Mabelle and Raj Arole. CRHP works to increase health awareness in rural areas and to raise the status of women in the community. More than half a million people in 400 villages have seen community health improve.

Five years later, 80 per cent of Tearfund's resources were still channelled through more than two dozen societies. Glyn Macaulay later recalled:

> The very early days were undoubtedly more missionary-orientated because we really did not have access to the indigenous church. It tended to be missionaries who became aware of Tearfund and applied for support.

This gave rise to a complex relationship. On the one hand some missionary societies saw Tearfund as diverting resources which might have come instead to them, but on the other, they found Tearfund a ready source of funding for projects they would otherwise have been unable to undertake. John Harvey, chairman of the Tearfund board from 1987 to 1990, recalled:

> Virtually everything was done through a mission society. Loads of people would be consulted as to whether they were a good society or not and whether they had good people, because there was always the question: Is this money going to a legitimate cause? In those early days building the network to find that out was quite hard, because we were starting from base zero.
>
> As soon as Tearfund got known, all the world descended on it,

particularly the mission societies who were struggling a bit for money. They began first of all to see Tearfund as a rival, but then also as a source of money for their projects, so it was a 'love-hate' relationship.

By contrast, for some in the missionary world Tearfund was definitely a welcome development that resonated with some of their own hopes and concerns – and enabled them to expand their own work. In 1974 *Tear Times* quoted Worldwide Evangelization Crusade (WEC) executive Neil Rowe:

> Some years ago there was a growing concern on the part of many WEC missionaries, especially in the poorer parts of Africa, to do more in a practical way to help the people to whom they were preaching the gospel. Some wanted to start simple agricultural schemes to help people who suffer from constant malnutrition. Others wanted to help in solving the growing problem of serious water shortage and water pollution. Others were concerned that the children they were teaching were growing up without hope of future employment and apparently condemned to a life of frustration and temptation. Schemes were being discussed but obviously much finance would be needed.

Tearfund's Annual Report 1973/74: As these pictures show, in the early days of Tearfund most of the people it worked with in developing countries were western missionaries and specialists who were committed to expressing Christian love in practical ways to poor and needy people.

Director's Report

PEOPLE WHO LOVE PEOPLE

"People... People who need people..." The words of the songwriter could well describe the people of the developing countries. People who are hungry and helpless and without hope – material and spiritual. And only people can meet their need. People who can transform their livelihood by sharing their skill; people who can transform their lives by sharing their faith.

Over the current financial year, Tear Fund are supporting over sixty such people in medical, agricultural, administrative and technological posts throughout the emerging nations, as well as forty "medics" who have been supported through our joint scheme with Reader's Digest.

Now, although all Tear Fund supported projects are carefully vetted and screened by some highly qualified medical, agricultural and building consultants, who apply their own respective criteria for checking the feasibility of each project, we have come to recognise that "God's method is God's man" is always a person. Someone who is burdened by the suffering of others. Someone with a vision to meet them at their point of need. Someone with a practical gift and skill to share and a meaningful faith to communicate. Someone who themselves has responded to, and now reflects, the love of Christ.

Even as I write, I have had a 'phone call from such a man. For the last three years we have been supporting him in his rehabilitation programme for Bengalis who lost their homes and their hope. For the last sixteen years this man has laboured amongst them. More recently he has seen the fruit of that labour as scores around him are responding to the love of the living Lord Jesus Christ that they see revealed in this man and his colleagues. Now his Land-Rover had packed up and needed some major replacements immediately... "Would Tear Fund be able to...?" I hadn't the slightest hesitation in encouraging him to obtain the necessary

parts at once (incidentally, his sigh of relief would have warmed the hearts of those whose gifts will put him back on the road).

I remember at an international consultation in Stuttgart a representative of the largest relief agency in Europe stating that money was not the problem in tackling the area under discussion. "If money was the answer" he remarked, "we could solve the problem." But he too realised that more important than the money that is spent is the men who spend the money – and their motivation. This so often determines the outcome of the programme and the project.

Looking at it from another angle, one Fleet Street journalist who toured the developing countries came to the conclusion that "Money can narrow the gap: only people can bridge it." We would endorse that conclusion. In fact, that's what led to the setting up of our overseas Personnel department last autumn, in order to match up the offers of service with the opportunities for service in the forty different countries where Tear Fund is involved. In the first six months our Overseas Personnel Secretary handled no less than 300 enquiries from a spectrum of qualified people.

We praise God then for these and all the other people we have the privilege of supporting. People who can help people – physically and spiritually. People who are marked and motivated by the love of God in Christ. People who love people.

REV. GEORGE HOFFMAN

1979: Vietnamese 'boat people' who had fled their country after the communist takeover receive food from Tearfund's partner PHILRADS (Philippine Relief and Development Services) in a refugee camp in the Philippines. As Tearfund moved away from working primarily with missionary societies in the 1970s and 1980s, some of the relationships it formed were with the relief and development arms of evangelical alliances – in this case, of the Philippine Council of Evangelical Churches.

I realised then that the emergence of Tear Fund could be God's way of making provision for such schemes. Since then, the WEC staff have been able to look into the whole matter and they feel that this is of God. Over the past years the Crusade has received many thousands of pounds for specific projects, such as digging wells, providing piped water supplies to large numbers of leprosy patients, starting agricultural projects, and so on.

We want to record our thanks to the Lord, to Tear Fund, and to the original donors for this provision. It is much more than just a financial transaction.

For above all, there is the real spiritual link. Tear Fund is certainly an agency handling money for relief work but it is motivated by true Christian compassion, and the end result is not just the alleviation of suffering but the glory of Christ.

The early 1970s brought a new development in Tearfund's working relationship with mission societies. On 8 January 1971 Robert Smith, Assistant General Secretary of the South American Missionary Society (SAMS), wrote to Tearfund saying that the provincial government in northern Argentina had assigned a considerable sum of money for the purpose of 'seeking to better the appalling social condition of the Indians in northern Argentina' and had invited Bishop David Leake to run the programme. Part of the scheme involved pumping muddy river water to farms and plantations for irrigation, however, and the letter noted that this 'pioneer task' would require someone with particular skills. It continued:

> S.A.M.S. feels they have found such a man in Mr Kevin McKemey to assist the Bishop in this vital task of meeting the immediate and pressing need for adequate irrigation, as well as allowing finance for the long-term help, that is preparing the Indians for the day in the near future when they could help themselves apart from the ex-patriate aid of money and manpower.
>
> The money entrusted to Bishop Leake for this big endeavour of help is only for the scheme itself and not for ex-patriate allowances, hence S.A.M.S. appeal to TEAR Fund for assistance in sending out the McKemeys.

Later that year 25-year-old Kevin McKemey and his wife Denise, an occupational therapist, together with fellow agriculturalists Peter and Frances Tyson, set off for the Chaco region of northern Argentina – the first people to be funded for overseas service by Tearfund. The connection worked with SAMS, no doubt, more than it might have with some other societies, because SAMS was particularly attuned to

Now you see us...

What Tearfund has contributed is very significant. We weren't into putting signs up saying 'This is a Tearfund building', and I don't think you were going to see a Tearfund flag flying over a project somewhere, because Tearfund was more about building up the national Christians. But we contributed, and something has grown as a result. I used to say we were like the Scarlet Pimpernel: now you see us, now you don't, but in the meantime something good was going on. We weren't there to tick off another convert: that's God's doing. But I think in eternity you will see a lot of people who have been influenced and won for Christ through Tearfund.

David Applin, Tearfund 1982–92

1971: Kevin and Denise McKemey (centre) and Peter and Frances Tyson (right) meet Bill Latham at Tearfund before starting their assignment in Argentina – the first people funded for overseas service by Tearfund.

the need for mission to include social action. The precise detail of who the young people 'belonged to', however, was subject to interpretation. Understandably, perhaps, Tearfund's publicity emphasised that Tearfund was financing the couples for their four-year assignment, whereas as far as SAMS – and the couples themselves – were concerned, they were going as SAMS missionaries. Kevin McKemey later recalled:

> My connection at that time was very much with SAMS. I viewed the Tearfund connection more as support to bolster the responsibility I had taken with SAMS rather than saying I was now a Tearfund employee. At that time, right at the beginning, that wasn't the way Tearfund was operating. It was offering support to missionary societies to support their personnel.

The undoubted empathy between Tearfund and this particular missionary society was to lead to major investment – the following year Tearfund launched its biggest single project yet: a £19,000 share in a ten-year programme of agricultural and medical development among the Chaco Indians.

The link with this work was also to prove a learning ground for Tearfund in its understanding of development. Ten years later, Kevin McKemey reflected in *Tear Times* on his years with what had become known as the Iniciativa Cristiana

Solution

  The only thing big enough to solve the problems of spiritual emptiness, selfish leadership, poverty, disease and ignorance is the network of millions of churches all around the world.

Rick Warren, Saddleback Valley Community Church, California, USA

programme. It was a bold attempt to tackle chronic social conditions and had made tremendous strides, with twenty-nine indigenous auxiliary nurses and health agents now established in the region, and the primary school initiated through the programme fully accepted by the local education council. He recognised, however, that the long-term economic development programmes had unconsciously created a dependency in the local communities, 'as we took on the complete responsibility for the needs of the area'. Those involved had also learnt something about their own limitations and the pitfalls of grandiose schemes. Looking to the future of Christian development work, he said:

It must begin with the local church, helping them to become strong and independent and alive to their own social needs, with the ability to respond to them.

I think in the past that Iniciativa Cristiana has been a body that offered a shoulder for the national church. Now the national church must take over from the 'missionary church' and be responsible for the governing and outworking of the Iniciativa Cristiana programme.

> Our desire is not that others might be relieved while you are hard pressed, but that there might be equality. At the present time your plenty will supply what they need, so that in turn their plenty will supply what you need. The goal is equality, as it is written: 'The one who gathered much did not have too much, and the one who gathered little did not have too little.' (2 Corinthians 8:13–15)

We will have to leave a structure, a programme of Christian action and social concern, that is within the local church's capacity to manage and is seen by those involved to be part of the local church and a true expression of their concern. And any external aid which comes to the area must be channelled through the local church, instead of by-passing it, as has happened in the past, causing confusion and misunderstanding.

Within Tearfund there was a growing realisation that the initiative had to lie with the local church rather than the missionary. In many countries, though the church was still comparatively young, indigenous leadership had emerged in parallel with a move away from dependence on foreign missions. Moreover, the local church was the body that would be there in the long term, and this was surely the most effective channel through which Christian involvement in social needs could be expressed. As early as 1969 this principle was articulated in the letter of invitation Tearfund sent to the missionary societies in advance of its November consultation with them:

A mother nurses her child during an epidemic in the Chaco region of Argentina in 1979. Tearfund's involvement in the Iniciativa Cristiana programme in this impoverished region was one of its major early commitments.

Recognising the new situation overseas and the changing pattern of partnership, Tear Fund believes that generally speaking the church or churches of a particular area should be the operative body, and not the missionary society. Projects must therefore be related to the life of the church, and not merely facilitate the activities of individual missionaries.

Other factors were also at work in what became for Tearfund a gradual shift from working through mission societies to establishing links with indigenous Christians. David Applin joined Tearfund in 1982 and was its Overseas Director from 1987 to 1992:

Early funding had gone through missions, because Tearfund was all the time dependent on people who knew things on the ground. It was also about relationships: George Hoffman had relationships with various church and mission leaders, and it was networking. But as the activity of indigenous groups grew, there was a desire to deal directly, not go through a third party, and rightly so. They wanted their leaders to have direct links with Tearfund.

Church

❝ The New Testament says the church is the body of Christ, but for the last hundred years, the hands and feet have been amputated, and the church has just been a mouth. And mostly, it's been known for what it's against. ❞
Rick Warren, Saddleback Valley Community Church, California, USA

Some of these people came knocking on Tearfund's door. I guess they must have read something in the publicity and thought, here's an evangelical agency that we can deal with. And at the same time, we began to expand into areas of the world where there were no missionaries we could work with anyway – for example, when there was an earthquake in Russia we formed a direct link with Moscow Baptist Church.

The first links with indigenous Christians were established as Tearfund staff came into contact with local evangelical leaders who were taking their own initiative in social action. One of these was Vijayan Pavamani, pastor of Emmanuel Church in Calcutta, who was a long-standing partner of Tearfund until his death in 2006. In 1978 he and his wife Premila opened a home for drug addicts, and in 1985 they opened another for homeless children where they could find rehabilitation, education and training. As Vijayan told *Tear Times* in 1978,

God is good

❝ Who I am as a person has been shaped by the people I have had the opportunity to meet through Tearfund. I met some women in a small business development project in Uganda who were helping to support one another. There were about twelve of them and their husbands had all died because of AIDS. They said they would like to pray and sing before we left. Most of them by now have probably been dead for some time, but they sang the song 'Yes God is good, yes, God is good', and I thought, of course I can say yes, God is good, because that is an objective truth. But then they sang, 'God is good to me' and I thought, in their situation would I be able to sing that the way they sang it? Seeing God's grace at work like that in people is a challenge to me. ❞
Jennie Collins, Tearfund 1992–2000

We have seen Christ do for individuals what years of treatment, medicine and hospitalisation could not do.

Such individuals were comparatively rare in the 1970s, however, and Tearfund sought to develop indigenous links at the national level too. Jennie Evans later recalled:

Vijayan Pavamani and his wife Premila. Vijayan was one of the first indigenous Christian leaders with whom Tearfund built a relationship in the 1970s, and he remained in partnership with Tearfund until his death in 2006. After opening their home to needy people from 1972, in 1978 Vijayan and Premila started a drug rehabilitation centre, the first in eastern India. In 1985 they opened the Pauline Bhawan home for street children. Tearfund's first chairman Glyn Macaulay said, 'Vijayan and Premila Pavamani became very much a part of our work at an early stage, because we got to know them and we trusted them.'

When I joined we were working with quite a discrete group of contacts overseas – I don't think we would have described them as partners at that point – and so if there was a disaster in any given situation, we would have contacts with someone or other, and there would be an ability to respond, albeit in a fairly modest way. So it was a fairly clear-cut, simple type of approach.

As we went on, little by little our link in development with the mission agencies here began to decrease and more and more we would have a direct contact with the church overseas. In Vietnam in 1975, for example, we were able to respond directly to the evangelical church there, while also working in conjunction with Project Vietnam Orphan, a UK-based agency. We made it a priority to develop direct links with the relief and development arms of evangelical alliances in other countries, such as EFICOR, the Evangelical Fellowship of India Commission on Relief. That moved us forward in some ways and we were able to make grants through these relief and development arms.

> ## Partners
> ❝ When we were starting out, Tearfund gave us space and opportunity – they took us as we were. As we developed and grew, the partnership has kept growing, and we have learnt a lot. Now we have partners of our own in the region, and we have a model: we want to treat our partners in the way we have been treated by Tearfund. ❞
> **Osvaldo Munguia, Director, Mopawi, Honduras**

> **Y**ou have been a refuge for the poor, a refuge for the needy in their distress. (Isaiah 25:4)

EFICOR started in 1967 as an evangelical Christian response to the drought and famine in Bihar State, and was known to early Tearfund supporters for its emergency relief and its well-drilling to provide safe drinking water. It later developed its capacity for disaster preparedness and mitigation work, and began to work in advocacy, defending the rights of the poorest. EFICOR has worked in fruitful partnership with Tearfund for the last four decades.

Tearfund's early willingness to put effort and energy into developing its relationships with indigenous Christian groupings bore considerable fruit. Its support enabled evangelical relief and development agencies to get established in a number of countries. Kevin McKemey recalled:

> ## Respect
> ❝ We appreciate Tearfund's advice and support. We like the way Tearfund works with partners like us, because they respect people. They respect our vision. They value our vision and they support it. ❞
> **Michel Kayitaba, Director, Moucecore, Rwanda**

This kind of activity by Tearfund really boomed during the 1970s and early 1980s. At that time, for me, looking at it from the partner side, Tearfund became an institution that was trusted by local churches, and it was seen to be one of the very few that actually trusted them. Having worked with a lot of other institutions over the years, I can say that that is one of the distinctives that Tearfund definitely had.

In some parts of the world, the emergence of a national church from under the wing of a missionary society would lead in itself to a direct relationship with Tearfund. Ethiopia was a case in point, as Jennie Evans recalled:

> The period of the Ethiopian famine in the 1970s was a very significant phase in this respect. We started our involvement there through the mission agency SIM, which was already giving birth to a national church. We very soon moved into a more direct relationship with this, the Kale Heywet Church, rather than working with a western-based NGO. It was a natural progression for us to partner with the local church, and I would say it was also quite significant in the way that we began to operate much more with locally based organisations.

The Kale Heywet Church became a long-standing partner of Tearfund, and Jennie recalled a moment when the nature of the partnership was expressed in a particularly compelling way, in 1994:

In the 1970s Tearfund helped to support EFICOR's programme drilling wells to provide water for poor communities in India.

Tearfund ran into some financial difficulties and when the Kale Heywet Church heard about it they actually gave us a substantial amount of money. That was very significant – not just that they had given us the money, which was lovely, but that they felt free to do that within the relationship they had with us. I'm not sure that some ten years previously that would necessarily have been the case. I think we would have been viewed as the donors and they as the recipients. But somehow that equality had come about, so that they could say, well, there's a need and we have the money and we will send it to them. It was wonderful.

Hope

" The local church is the hope of the world. "

Bill Hybels, Willow Creek Community Church, Chicago, USA

Through the 1980s and 1990s the concept of partnership developed and grew. At its heart was that desire to move from the model of western 'giver' and developing

2006: When drought caused famine in northern Kenya, Tearfund's local church partners were able to distribute emergency food supplies to the most vulnerable people. For Tearfund, the local church is the key to physical and spiritual transformation in poor communities.

Opposite: Ethiopia's Kale Heywet Church has brought clean water to many villages, saving women the back-breaking daily task of fetching it from rivers, streams and springs sometimes far from home.

world 'receiver' to one that more fully recognised the equality of both sides in the relationship.

In Guinea Bissau, for example, in the 1970s Tearfund provided the salary of a British WEC worker, and then sent other expatriates (mostly nurses) through WEC. In the 1980s, how-ever, Tearfund began to second people directly to the Evangelical Church of Guinea Bissau, who themselves trained the church's staff. Here, as in other parts of the world, the result was a considerable strengthening in the capacity of the indigenous church to manage its own programmes. When civil war broke out in Guinea Bissau in the late 1990s, the church was able to run a displaced persons operation for the World Food Programme without direct expatriate involvement.

> In all my prayers for all of you, I always pray with joy because of your partnership in the gospel from the first day until now, being confident of this, that he who began a good work in you will carry it on to completion until the day of Christ Jesus. (Philippians 1:4–6)

Under Doug Balfour's leadership as General Director from 1995 to 2004 Tearfund reshaped itself internally in pursuit of teamwork and a flatter, less hierarchical structure, and this think-ing spilled over into the organisa-tion's international relationships. Concrete steps included appointing regional advisers in developing coun-tries, who were national Christians rather than UK expatriates, and whose role was to provide advice and support to partners in those countries. Doug Balfour later recalled:

United

66 Tearfund is very much committed to the Christian mandate, to biblical values – that's evident in its core values. And that's what I like the most about Tearfund, because you can be united in heart, united in the Bible, and go out together with the same heart. I also value the servant leadership within Tearfund. Over the years I've always found Tearfund people are willing to share, to help people understand, and to learn from them. That's not true of all organisations in my experience, so I value that very much. 99

Philippe Ouedraogo, Director, AEAD, Burkina Faso

> We thought that having a local person based in-region would add a lot of understanding and credibility to our work with partners, particu-larly in the area of capacity-building. Our first appointment was Prince David, in India, who became a role model for what was possible – we realised regional advisers were a good investment in terms of connect-ing with local partners and of decentralising decision-making.

In Jennie Evans' view, recent years have seen a marked change in the nature of the relationship between Tearfund and its partners:

> I think there is much more consultation now, and there is a greater freedom on the part of partners to engage in dialogue. We try to ensure we're not the sole donor for any one programme, because we don't want to create any kind of dependency on Tearfund, but at the same time there is a depth of relationship with many of the partners that gives them the freedom to tell us when they disagree, and to have a lively debate. There is an increased confidence on their part, a recognition that we are all players in the same field and we have different skills and abilities and gifts to bring, to complement one another.

Bangladesh, 2002: In the slums of Dhaka, Tearfund's partner HEED paid teenage girls like Lipi (pictured centre) a small wage to teach younger children – bringing free education to the youngsters and enabling the girls to pay for their own continuing education.

The 1990s also saw a greater emphasis in Tearfund on building up the partner organisations' own strengths – through training, discussion and sharing of expertise, increasing their ability and capacity to work with poor communities and bring lasting change. The aim was not just to help partners achieve more impact, but also to ensure they became less dependent on Tearfund, as Jennie Collins, Tearfund's International Director from 1992 to 2000, later recalled:

You can have a great relationship between the heads of two organisations, but the question is, how sustainable are the programmes or the organisation once the leader moves on? The important thing is for the organisation to carry a vision for bringing about change, to be clear about what that vision is, and for its work to be sustainable.

Tearfund started out with personal relationships and grants of money, but then we realised that for partners to be really able to use this money to do the things they wanted to do, we needed to give attention not just to technical input, such as how to dig a well better, but also to how does this organisation run, what's its focus, what are its financial and personnel systems, and those sort of things. We needed to develop relationships in such a way that there was an involvement in building the capacity of organisations. I think that was a big change that happened over time.

In 2005 Tearfund took partnership to a new level when it created a 'Partner panel', a group of overseas partners who were to convene once a year with Tearfund leaders in order to discuss and influence Tearfund's strategy. Doug Balfour, then Tearfund's chief executive, recalled:

> The idea was to give our partners a voice in the way we ran the whole organisation, to recognise them as key stakeholders and to hear their perspective, because it was often different from our own perspective but really important.

A savage civil war throughout the 1990s and into the new century left thousands of Liberians traumatised, bereaved and homeless. Mulbah Zayzay (pictured) was one of up to 10,000 people living in a camp for displaced people on the outskirts of the capital, Monrovia, where Tearfund's partner the Association of Evangelicals of Liberia (AEL) provided emergency help. AEL built toilets, wells and bathhouses, gave public health training, and worked in trauma counselling and reconciliation. AEL's General Secretary Beyan Bakai said, 'There's a lot of hurt in this country. We need to expose people to scripture and joy so that they can forgive one another, like I've forgiven the Muslims who killed my parents.'

Grass roots

So much Western aid has had no impact in eradicating poverty because the poor people have not been involved. Rich nations meet governments in poor countries and discuss how to deal with poverty at an international and national level. But for aid to have an impact the people at the grass roots must be involved. They have a role to play too.

We must find ways of improving partnership so that our intervention forces poverty backwards. As a church we have been sent out by God to proclaim the gospel of love.

Archbishop Donald Mtetemela, head of Diocese of Ruaha Integrated Development Programme, Tanzania

Bolivia, 2001: In the city of Cochabamba, Tearfund's partner Mosoj Yan helped street girls to find a new life, offering practical, emotional and spiritual support.

For Dino Touthang, Executive Director of EFICOR and a member of the Partner panel, his organisation's long-standing partnership with Tearfund has been a blessing and an encouragement:

I think Tearfund's sharing with the global church has been tremendous. There's a tendency for resource organisations to dictate, but with Tearfund there's a rare environment of listening to one another. I definitely see an effort and a willingness to listen and to keep asking, Can we do it better? That is a spirit that I really love about Tearfund.

Chapter 5

Doing Development

What is development? A 1976 Tearfund poster asking this question offered the following answer: 'Development is about people. It is about life. It is about giving people the opportunity to live as God intended.'

It was a simple definition, but caught the heart of Tearfund's vision, seeing development as people-focused and about the quality of life that God intended his creatures to have. This conviction has remained central to Tearfund's work – but there have been many lessons along the way. Today, Tearfund has grown into a respected and

Thailand, 1997: Tearfund partner the Issaan Development Foundation was helping poor farmers to increase their food supply and income by fishing as part of its work in north-east Thailand.

Darkness to light

❝ We've been working in a community in the north-west of Nepal. It's just fantastic. Already there's a church of about twenty people there, and that has happened because the people have seen what's happening and then they ask the questions. It so often works that way round.

I went to the grand opening of the toilets in this community, and the children had written poems. They said, 'We have come from darkness to light. Nobody cared for us, nobody came to see us; the leaders only came when they wanted votes.' They sang this and the little girls danced to it, and then they said, 'Then UMN came, and they cared for us and they loved us.' That is what Tearfund is about. ❞

Jennie Collins, Tearfund 1992–2000, Executive Director, United Mission to Nepal (UMN), 2000–

professional international development agency, with a wealth of experience, skill and expertise in development: the fruits of a forty-year journey of learning.

At the beginning it was fairly straightforward. As original committee member Peter Meadows recalled,

> It was essentially relief work in those days, because the concept of development, helping whole communities find their own future, was hardly there. It was a lot of 'do-gooding' really, and providing resources for Christians at the front line who knew they had to do the gospel in word and deed, so that they could do the 'deed' bit.

Tearfund was, to quote the words of one early staff member, 'like a grant-making trust', oriented mainly towards sending comparatively small amounts of money for emergency relief. Very soon, however, it found itself increasingly involved in longer-term development – working with poor individuals, families and communities to improve their lives. By 1973, 80 per cent of its aid was allocated to long-term development projects, with agricultural schemes and public health programmes the most prominent.

> You, Lord, hear the desire of the afflicted; you encourage them, and you listen to their cry, defending the fatherless and the oppressed.
> (Psalm 10:17–18)

Why did this happen? It was a recognition that while a 'quick fix' is necessary in emergencies, lasting solutions to the problems of a poor community require longer-term action. As a later *Tear Times* front cover put it, the world 'needs more than a sticking plaster'. Tearfund was committed to caring for the sick, for example, but its

main thrust had to be in prevention rather than cure – investing in improving water supplies and sanitation, hygiene and housing, and training village health workers who could give basic health education.

In the early years, Tearfund's theory of development was simple. It was fond of quoting the saying 'Give a man a fish, and he will eat for a day. Teach him how to fish, and he will eat for the rest of his life.' In 1970, *Tear Times* confidently proclaimed that this 'old Chinese proverb' was 'what development, or self help, is all about'. As Tearfund's Dewi Hughes pointed out twenty-eight years later in his book *God of the poor*, however, even this simple saying conceals a somewhat paternalistic assumption:

> The implication is that the poor are ignorant – they don't know how to fish – so they need someone to come along and teach them how to do it. Fundamental to this approach is the conviction that the West knows best. Development means the transference of western ways of doing things. The poor need to be trained to do things in the western way so that they can escape from poverty.

A mission's programme in Nigeria was held up as an example of the 'teach a man to fish' principle and described as 'one of the most

By investing in health education workers, Tearfund and its partners have brought life-saving health, hygiene and sanitation advice to poor communities.

Priority

❝ Our priority as Christians is not the amount that can be harvested nor the profit that a person or a group can make. It is the total welfare – spiritual, social, mental, economic – of the greatest number of people. ❞
Peter Batchelor, *People in Rural Development*, 1993

imaginative projects submitted to Tear Fund'. It employed Nigerian tailors to provide clothing for victims of the country's recent war using locally manufactured cloth – a way of helping the local economy as well as providing relief. By later standards, however, it would be found lacking: the cloth was bought using money from Tearfund and other overseas agencies, rendering the project dependent on

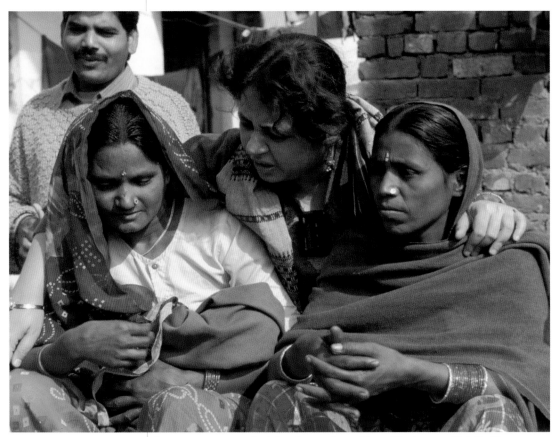

'It was not my own decision. It was the calling of God on my life': Dr Kiran Martin began working in the slums of Delhi in 1988. Tearfund worked in partnership with her organisation Asha (the Hindi word for hope) from its earliest days. With a vision to empower the slum residents, Asha trained women to be volunteer health workers and worked with the community to provide clinics and to improve water supplies and sanitation. Asha also worked with the authorities to secure land rights for the slum-dwellers. By 2007, Asha was transforming the lives of more than a quarter of a million slum-dwellers in forty-five slum colonies around the city, and health statistics in the slums where Asha worked were better than those for India as a whole.

external funding and so not self-sustaining in the long term.

Like all growing organisations, Tearfund had to go through changes. The original committee and the early staff were talented, highly motivated and compassionate people, keen to see Christians demonstrate a practical response to suffering and need. But without professional field experience in development, they had limited knowledge of what would be likely to work and what would not.

They had a small number of consultants on whom they could call for advice, but in the early 1980s it was recognised that more in-house professional expertise was required to help those responsible for deploying Tearfund's resources. The answer was to create a team of in-house consultants with extensive overseas medical, agricultural and development experience: John Townsend, Ian Wallace and Kevin McKemey, who together were known within Tearfund as the 'Three Wise Men'. Their appointment was significant, as Jennie Evans recalled:

> Before this, there was nothing actually written down in terms of what we should fund, so they helped us to formulate a strategy and criteria that we could work with. It was a major change. For us it was a real Godsend because it brought a quality to our own understanding, brought credibility into our process, and also benefited our partners in terms of the quality of their work. I think the whole understanding of development in Tearfund came about largely because of John and Ian and Kevin being in-house. And from that we began to develop a much wider network of technical consultants who could help us in different areas.

This step laid the foundation for a process of professionalisation that would continue over the following decades. It was a turning point, enabling Tearfund to build up its understanding of both the theory and practice of development.

The period of the 'Three Wise Men' also saw the creation of Tearfund's *Footsteps* magazine. Originally known as *Footsteps to Health*, it was first published in 1986 under Joy Poppe's editorship and

Self-development

A man is not being developed if someone gives things to him. A man develops himself by what he does. He develops himself by making his own decisions; by increasing his own knowledge and ability, and by his own full participation as an equal in the life of the community he lives in.

People cannot be developed, they can only develop themselves.

Julius Nyerere, President of Tanzania 1964–85, quoted by George Hoffman in *Third Way* magazine, 1982

TRANSPORT

Bicycle trailers

BICYCLES are found all over the world and are a very useful way of transporting people and loads. The use of a motor vehicle may often be impossible for a variety of reasons – usually because of the high cost, and sometimes because there are few accessible roads. Without transport it is very difficult to carry quantities of goods to market. Adapting bicycles to carry loads more effectively can bring great benefits.

Baskets or paniers can be added to a bicycle. Even more useful are small trailers. These may be expensive to buy ready-made, but here are some good ideas to help build your own at very little cost. These designs have all been tested and proved useful. Once the main frame is built, you can adapt their design for your own purposes, depending on your priorities – a tanker to carry water, an open trailer to carry goods, a flat bed trailer to use as an ambulance to carry sick people – there are all sorts of possibilities. You may want more than one kind of

trailer. If bicycles are very expensive, a group of farmers could join together and buy a bicycle and trailer which could be available for each of them in turn. In urban areas, trailers could be used for a variety of means of earning income – such as selling vegetables, paraffin or charcoal, distributing drinking water or rubbish collection. In towns and cities, however, heavy motor traffic may be a hazard.

If you become skilled in producing these trailers, they could also prove a useful source of income if you are able to sell them.

Recommended reading…

The Design of Cycle Trailers, by M Ayre. Cost £8.50 from Intermediate Technology Development Group.

ITDG
Myson House
Railway Terrace
Rugby
CV21 4HT
UK

Box trailer

This design was developed by Ben Maxted in Sri Lanka and the joint is bolted onto the back luggage rack, allowing the trailer to roll on rough surfaces without damage.

The basic trailer was adapted by Mallavi Hospital and converted into a covered ambulance. This could carry one person – sitting or lying down, with a tray at the front for carrying health materials. The roof provided shade for the patient.

This design was made from welded tube steel which is not too expensive in Sri Lanka. A bending machine is useful as it reduces the amount of welding needed and gives a stronger frame. You may want to use thicker diameter tubing.

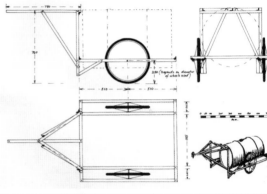

Towing link detail

Flat bed trailer

This design was developed by Ken Hargesheimer and bolts onto the bike frame just above the back wheel. Although this design could also be made from welded metal, not many people have metal welding equipment. This frame has therefore been made either from angle iron or wood – drilling holes in the end of each piece and bolting the frame together. It may also be possible to make a frame out of bamboo – tightly tied together at the joints.

Towing link detail

Ken Hargesheimer
PO Box 1901
Lubbock
TX 79408-1901
USA

Watch where you're going!

Certain driving skills are needed to drive a trailer, which is, of course, much wider than a bicycle. Allow plenty of room for driving round corners and beware of holes in the road. Don't overload these trailers – both designs should carry up to 100 kg, or a little more if they are made out of metal. Used with care, they should provide many years of useful service.

14   FOOTSTEPS No.21

FOOTSTEPS No.21   15

---

produced regularly for two years until Joy left to work in Nepal. After a gap it was revived in 1989, when Isabel Carter, an agriculturalist who had worked for Tearfund in Kenya, was appointed editor. Retitled *Footsteps*, it broadened its focus to embrace all aspects of development. From the 1,000 copies of the first issue in 1986 it has grown to 50,000 copies per issue, and it is produced in seven languages.

The aim of *Footsteps* is to share good practice, information and ideas. It keeps local health and development workers particularly in mind, so it works hard to be practical and to keep the language

Footsteps

❝ One of the best things Tearfund does is *Footsteps*. Even if it didn't do anything else, *Footsteps* would probably be the best capacity-building tool. You find it in more places than anything else. ❞
Bill Crooks, Tearfund 1993–2002

Children and HIV

In Cambodia, Tearfund partner Servants to Asia's Urban Poor cares for hundreds of families affected by HIV and AIDS in the slums of the capital, Phnom Penh. Medical and nutritional support can help prolong the lives of affected people. One young mother whose husband had died of an AIDS-related illness and who was now ill herself said:

'If it wasn't for Servants, I probably wouldn't have anything to eat. They feed my children; they feed me. They give me medicine – and listen to me every day. When they pray with me I feel peace in my heart. I feel happier. I can sometimes sleep at night.'

Local church members provide most of the project's home care workers and the youth volunteers who act as 'big brothers or sisters' to orphans, befriending them, playing with them and taking them on outings. All this work is integrated into wider programmes for community nutrition, immunisation and general healthcare. 'Our goal,' say Servants, 'is to show the love of Christ in the midst of a devastating pandemic.'

accessible for people who are reading it in a second language or who haven't had the benefit of much education. Every issue has included a Bible study to relate the Bible's teaching to the issues of everyday development work. Twenty years on, *Footsteps* was reaching into every corner of the world, said Isabel Carter:

Nigeria, 2005: Tearfund partner the Fellowship of Christian Students gave HIV awareness talks in schools across twenty of Nigeria's states, reaching 2 million children.

The philosophy is to make it available to anyone who can use it. It's had fantastic impact for Tearfund. It's been a way of sharing Tearfund's expertise in a very gentle way with a vast number of organisations, and it's had a huge impact in the development world in ways that possibly will never be measured. So many people say years later that they've followed its advice, whether it was on setting up grain banks, or microfinance, or any other aspect of development. For example, someone in Uganda took a simple design we'd published for a bicycle trailer and set up a huge business producing bicycle ambulances so that sick or injured people in villages could be easily carried to the nearest medical help.

Tearfund started in an age when the dominant idea in development was

Process

❝ Development is always a process, never just a specific project. ❞
D. Merrill Ewert

2000: Families in Tangaye village, Burkina Faso, were unable to work all their drought-hardened earth because they could only till it by hand. When the meagre harvest ran out they would face months of hunger. The local church set up a village development committee, and with support from Tearfund and its local church partner AEAD a scheme was started to provide families with oxen for ploughing. As a result, people could cultivate more land and grow more food.

Community

In the north of Kenya, on the border with Sudan and Ethiopia, there's a very remote place where the church has done a really good job with the community, which is largely Muslim, building catchment dams because the area is so dry. When the drought got really bad the local Muslim population received a food distribution from an Islamic aid agency, on condition that it was used for Muslims only – but they said we must give it to the Christians too, because they've done such a great job with us and they're our brothers and sisters.

Bill Crooks, Tearfund 1993–2002

'big is beautiful': major programmes, large investments, advanced technology. The assumption was that if poor countries were to develop, they needed an injection of the technological resources on which western economic prosperity was founded. Early Tearfund projects, for example, included the construction of a large hydro-electric dam. Later, however, questions were raised about the effectiveness of solutions that were imposed from outside or overly dependent on technology. Tearfund's second Ian Wallace (not the one mentioned above), who worked in Sudan and Guinea Bissau for the organisation in the 1980s and later became its International Operations Director, reflected on this early view:

> We were the Blue Peter generation: 'If we collect enough bottle tops for a tractor and send it out to Africa, everything will be sorted. They'll have this machine that will enable them to develop.' We used to think like that: it was about transferring wealth and injecting resources, and that was our responsibility. Within the newly independent countries of Africa there was the dream of becoming a modern industrialised nation, and everyone thought we could just transfer the machinery to them and stick it in the ground and it would happen.
>
> I think we've all grown a lot wiser, and realised that actually the resource is not the key element in tackling poverty: it's much more about helping people to develop their own sense of vision, to work together, to identify their own resources and do what they can, regardless of what might be happening elsewhere, and then if possible to try to supplement that. So it's been a shift in emphasis.

He raises the poor from the dust and lifts the needy from the ash heap. (Psalm 113:7)

Tearfund began to think more in terms of working with poor communities, listening to their own perception of their needs and

The challenge of HIV and AIDS

Tearfund has worked for many years with church-based volunteers who provide support to people affected by HIV and AIDS, motivated by Christian compassion. As Uganda's Bishop Misaeri Kauma wrote in *Tear Times* in 1991, 'God is a friend of people who are in trouble, who have forgotten the answer. He wants to be their answer, their future, their hope.'

Recognising as the new century started that the virus was undoing decades of development work in poor communities, Tearfund made tackling HIV a top priority in all its work. In 2006 it launched a major campaign, *Work a miracle*, to help stop the spread of HIV, in particular curbing its transmission from mothers to babies. At the same time a Tearfund report, *Faith untapped*, drew attention to the 'untold story': the huge and growing network of churches tending the sick, caring for orphans and wrestling to halt the spread of infection at grass-roots level, reaching the people and communities that governments cannot easily reach. The experience of Tearfund's partners in Uganda and other countries had shown that the church has a crucial role to play in the battle against HIV and AIDS.

Above: In 2006 Esther, from Malawi, was one of 17.3 million women living with HIV. She and her daughter Alinafe helped Tearfund to highlight the risks of mother-to-child transmission of HIV by appearing in Tearfund's film *Work a miracle*.

Education is vital in helping families and communities to break out of poverty. Many of Tearfund's partners run schools for children who would otherwise have no chance of an education: here it was the evangelical Meserete Kristos Church in Ethiopia that in 1998 brought schools to a poor rural area that had never had any, in response to a request by the local community. Frehiwot, the church's education co-ordinator, said, 'In just two short years, the changes have been really amazing.'

priorities, moving from a directive to a participative approach. It was also influenced by the general move in the development world in the 1970s to the 'small is beautiful' perspective, inspired by the writings of E.F. Schumacher, in particular his book *Small is beautiful: economics as if people mattered*, published in 1973.

Writing in *Third Way* magazine in 1982, George Hoffman noted that over the previous ten years 'the strongest single influence on our understanding of development' had been the thinking and teaching of Schumacher. *Small is beautiful* advocated decentralised, small-scale, local development and the application of 'intermediate technology' – tools and other equipment that could easily be made and used in poor places.

Tearfund, he wrote, had also learnt in its first ten years that 'bigger' did not necessarily mean 'better'. Grandiose projects might promise to remedy all sorts of problems, but they could be expensive to implement and difficult for the local population to sustain. Smaller projects had the advantage of being more easily manageable, particularly as in these early years Tearfund still thought in terms of introducing western expertise and 'handing it on' to the indigenous people.

Two other key issues began to feature in Tearfund's thinking at this time. If a development project were proposed, would it merely tackle the symptoms, or would it address the source of the problem? And would the project be sustainable, or would it be for ever dependent on outside support?

Part of this was Tearfund's gradual move away from 'welfare' projects that dispensed goods to needy individuals. Looking back later on the welfare approach, Jennie Evans explained:

> We began to see it was a bottomless pit. It was providing short-term interventions but not actually dealing with the longer-term causes. It was quite short-sighted, and so over a period of time we began to say

Restoration

❝ God has a plan for restoration – to restore the needy, restore the sorrowful, restore those who have suffered injustice. If we have the opportunity to play a role in that, we have to do it. It is really a privilege. ❞

Osvaldo Munguia, Director, Mopawi, Honduras

Wells of salvation

❝ By the end of my four years working with the Evangelical Church of Guinea Bissau we had a projects office that really gave the church more of a sense of substance and stability: it wasn't just about the pastors running churches; the church was able to play its part more fully in life. There was an area in northern Guinea Bissau where we'd been doing hand-dug wells. The villagers helped to dig the well; they collected the sand and gravel and we provided the cement and the forming rings.

We also provided a foreman who would live in the village for six weeks and work with them to dig the well. When I visited six or seven years later, in every single village where we'd dug a well there was now a church where there hadn't been one before. It was very interesting that just the foreman living in the village and talking about why he was doing it was the seed that planted the church. The church has spread rapidly throughout that northern part of the country. ❞

Ian Wallace, Tearfund 1996–2007

Thailand, 2005: The South Asia tsunami of December 2004 left mental as well as physical scars – nine-year-old Nan was one of many children who survived the water but were left traumatised. Tearfund's partner Siam Care provided counsellors such as Ying, pictured here with Nan, as part of its response to the disaster.

Tearfund works with the local church to strengthen its capacity to change people's lives. When the resources of the church are mobilised, it can bring significant transformation. Here, church members help to build up the land around their church building so it can act as a place of shelter for local people during floods.

actually this is not really a priority for us. That doesn't mean we'll never do it, because there will always be a need for welfare, but we ask ourselves what can we do not just to address the immediate need but also perhaps to bring people out of that situation. So for example, if children aren't able to get education, rather than just making funds available to allow a certain number to attend school, we ask why the parents can't address the issue themselves. If it turns out that they can't because they haven't got work, we try to do something about that.

This is quite a change from Tearfund's early days, when we would make welfare grants to vitiate the situation as it was, but not actually delve further back. It's been part of a natural progression in Tearfund.

The questions of tackling underlying problems, listening to local people's needs and ensuring the sustainability of projects were all fundamental, and interlinked. Putting these principles into practice was of course challenging, and in this, as in many other areas, Tearfund's experience has been based on learning by doing: taking action, then reflecting on its positive and negative aspects and

refining the action the next time round – or to put it simply, learning by its mistakes.

As Tearfund marked its fifteenth anniversary, *Tear Times* chose to illustrate its work with a feature about a project among the Maasai people in Kenya, which it called 'an imaginative experiment in rural development'. Kenya's Anglican Church, in partnership with the Church Missionary Society (CMS) and Tearfund, had decided to try to respond to the Maasai's needs, and in 1983 it was a success story. The vicar of Narok township and a CMS missionary set up eight parish Growth Centres which would help the Maasai to help

> For we are God's handi-work, created in Christ Jesus to do good works, which God prepared in advance for us to do.
> (Ephesians 2:10)

UK, 2003: As part of Tearfund's UK Action programme, church-based partner groups in various parts of the UK provided vital counselling, support and friendship for refugees and asylum-seekers.

themselves physically, morally and spiritually. Avoiding the mistake of assuming that they knew best, the two men started by asking the Maasai elders what assistance they would like.

In one location, the answer was nursery education for their children and better health for their cattle. In response, the Christians put up a building to serve as a school, church and meeting room, installed a pump at the river to supply water to the building and to a cattle dip, provided a teacher and appointed a field worker/evangelist to look after and run the dip. The project was successful, with healthier herds and educated children, showing that partnership

On the front line

❝ Working in a famine situation, there were times when I woke up in the morning and got out of my sleeping bag and thought, 'There is no way I can go back into that. There is no way I can be positive and work as though this is going to arrive at a better outcome.' Sometimes there are no answers. You just have to trust that God does have a plan, and although you may never see the end of it, it is there somewhere and you just have to do your bit of it and leave the rest in his hands.

I used to have a sign on my mud hut that I looked at as I went out – it just said, 'I can't but You can, so let's go.' That got me through a lot of things – it was recognising that actually I couldn't go out and immerse myself in it all again, but I knew God could and he had hold of me, so together we just got on with it.

I've found that where I would likely draw the line and opt out, God will kind of draw alongside me and encourage me and give me a boot up the backside and say, 'Come on, we can do a bit more here.' I guess that is what keeps me going. ❞

Sue Mills, Tearfund 1973–

between the local church, missionary enterprise and concerned Christians in the UK could be effective. Tearfund's then chairman Simon Webley, who had visited the project, wrote:

> There are no quick solutions but by identifying the needs, listening to their ideas and then participating with them in their own development, providing where appropriate, people, know-how and money we can offer practical love and the good news of Jesus.

In later years, however, the project ran into trouble. Ian Wallace recalled that on a visit to the project he was told that once Tearfund stopped providing a nurse to work in the clinic that had been built, it fell into disrepair, as did the original cattle dip. It seemed the project had proved too dependent on outside support.

The issue of dependency was a key factor in moving forward Tearfund's development thinking in the 1990s and into the new century. Experience had shown that for a development programme to be sustainable, injecting external resources was not enough: it needed ownership of the project at the local level, and the ability to manage it. Tearfund's response was to set up a partner training post in 1993, recruiting Bill Crooks, who embarked on a series of training workshops with partners:

The idea was to build up our partners' capacity. Essentially, that's about helping them to be better organisations so they can do what they want to do much better. For Tearfund this was a move away from being mainly a funding body and towards helping partners to be more effective in their programmes. We brought partners together from different countries and continents to share experience and learning, and I think for many of them it was quite significant to network and find out what others were doing, and to feel encouraged and spiritually uplifted. Tearfund played quite an interesting catalytic role in this.

Capacity-building in this way became an important strategy for Tearfund. It included helping partner organisations to develop the leadership, structures and skills that would enable them to use money and resources well and to be as effective as possible in bringing change to vulnerable communities. With strengthened capacity, their work would be more sustainable and less dependent on external support.

The local church is at the heart of Tearfund's work to help people overcome poverty. As part of its community, the local church is the most effective agent of transformation, and is often the driving force for development.

Bolivia, 2005: Eight-year-old René tastes a tomato for the first time in his life. High in the Andes mountains, poor Quechua communities suffer malnutrition for lack of vitamins. Tearfund's partner Yanapanakuna started working with them to eradicate the problem. Now families grow fruit and vegetables in simple mud-walled greenhouses and their children are healthier. Pastor Julian is part of the team and shares the Bible's teaching on relationships between God, people and the environment. Fausto, a parent, says, 'My father told me the Word of God, but it was Yanapanakuna who taught me the meaning of it.'

There was still some way to go, however, in achieving development done by and through the church and the community, as opposed to by an external agency. For Tearfund, the next step forward in this respect came from a more unexpected source: its work with the church in the UK.

From the beginning Tearfund had used a small part of its resources to support church-based projects in the UK addressing poverty. As early as 1971 a grant was approved for a mission-run rehabilitation centre in London and over the years that followed, while there was no specific strategy for work in the UK, occasional grants were made to various projects. In 1996, however, Tearfund linked up with the Evangelical Alliance to launch a major initiative: UK Action. The aim was to help evangelical Christians in the UK to find ways of helping poorer communities at home. Tearfund Deputy Director Graham Fairbairn recalled:

> At this time there was a growing awareness of the social deprivation in our own society. Supporters kept saying to us, 'Charity begins at home: what are you doing in the UK?' and it got to the point where, with the EA, we felt that we needed to do something in the UK context. Some of us took some persuasion about how big UK Action should become: for example, would it compete with our main calling to work overseas? The decisive factor for me was that our work in the UK could be informed by our international work. Our partners overseas had a lot they could teach churches in the UK about working with the poor.

UK Action was later incorporated into Tearfund's mainstream work, as the organisation continued to help churches in the UK engage with poverty on their own doorstep. It developed *Church, Community and Change*, a process based on the experience and learning of some of Tearfund's overseas partners, which helped UK churches to understand the needs of people around them. It emphasised that a church's attitudes and culture could be as important as resources in making a development project successful. Instead of the church deciding what people in the community needed, it should talk to them and help them to set the agenda, to which the church could then respond.

In God's providence, this in turn proved to be a useful tool for helping churches in the developing world to engage in more sustainable development, when it formed the basis of a Tearfund process called Church and Community Mobilisation. This process encouraged the church and the community to develop a vision for the future, and then to identify what resources they already had that could be applied to pursuing that vision. The result was genuine local ownership of the vision and the solutions, and a commitment to moving forward without dependence on external support: Tearfund's input was typically small financial contributions and ongoing training. The process recognised and reinforced the role of the local church at the heart of community transformation.

Kenya, 2003: Tearfund partner the Narok Integrated Development Programme has worked alongside its local Maasai community to help them realise their goal of increased food security. Now the people can store enough maize to see them through lean times.

This approach was applied in the Narok development programme, and as Ian Wallace found, the mobilisation of both church and community turned it round:

This was done very much at local level with the local church. It was about the vision of the local people for their village. They did drawings of their vision of the village in thirty years' time, and they were then challenged to look at their own resources and make their own plans. As a result of that they went and refenced the clinic compound, painted it, replaced the glass, cut the grass, then got a nurse from Nairobi to come out and work in the clinic.

All of this was done through the local Christian community, and it's very exciting what's going on there. I think this typifies something of the change not just in Tearfund, but also to some extent in development thinking, a move away from the top-down external injection of resources and towards local involvement, local ownership. It's also about the presence of Christ being there in that community, and the followers of Christ being the people who are leading the way in terms of this vision of a newer, brighter future.

In more recent years, the Narok Integrated Development Programme (NIDP) has continued successfully. It has helped the community to withstand food shortages by building maize stores. In December 2005 famine struck, and the Kenyan government began distributing relief food in the district, but none of the areas served by NIDP needed it: they had enough food in store to see them through. Bill Crooks evaluated the project in 2005:

The results are phenomenal. As a result of the Church and Community Mobilisation process, the Maasai people are building earth dams with their hands on a scale you just can't believe, and livestock rates are rocketing: it's just massive change. I don't think I've ever seen a project in my entire development life that has achieved such large-scale infrastructural changes, and also some quite brave things, such as raising funds by selling cattle, which was almost unheard of, and moving into bee-keeping, which was not their culture.

Another project where they've used this approach to mobilise the church – in the Mount Kenya East district – shows equally remarkable results. The church has gone to the community, saying, 'This is something we really feel passionate about. Do you want to work with us on this?'

Opposite: Globally, by 2005 an estimated 12.5 million children had lost one or both parents to AIDS. Some 80 per cent of these children – about 12 million – lived in sub-Saharan Africa. In many cases, children had to take over as head of their household with no adults to look after them. In Uganda in 2007, Rachel (centre), 13, was acting as parent to six children orphaned by AIDS.

Crisis

The HIV and AIDS crisis is no longer just a development issue: it is a global disaster.
Tearfund report *Faith untapped*, 2006

Opposite: Southern Sudan, 1976: Agriculturist Roger Sharland was one of many specialists seconded to ACROSS through Tearfund's STOP programme.

ACROSS (the Africa Committee for Rehabilitation of Southern Sudan) – was set up in 1972 by Tearfund and four evangelical missions. It engaged in emergency relief work for the suffering population and in training for medical, agricultural and educational services. In 2007 the organisation, now known as Across, marked thirty-five years of serving the people of southern Sudan as the country suffered war, famine and poverty, and it continued to build local skills in the church and the community.

Resist

❝❝ We have to resist the seductive pull of colonial attitudes in which we arrogantly assume the right to inject our technocratic solutions into environments where they do not apply, and we must fight the paternalistic 'we-know-what-is-best-and-can-solve-your-problems-for-you' stance which still plays a part in motivating the support which many give to relief and development causes. ❞❞

Morgan Derham, *Tear Times,* **1987**

and it's created an incredible sense of unity, of churches working together and the community respecting the church. The result is a much stronger church and total transformation of communities – incredible change.

The other interesting thing is that they use the Bible a lot, and when you talk to people they say, 'Well, the great thing about the Bible is that we've seen that some of this stuff has been done before, so we're not scared.' When secular agencies come and try to do the same kind of thing they don't really know where it's coming from or going, but once you've got the Bible there it gives a really good basis of common understanding and a common language which we're familiar with.

Tearfund's long process of learning about development has benefited from another rich vein of input – the experience of its overseas workers. Specialists in agriculture, water engineering, health, nutrition and other skills, they have worked alongside Tearfund partner groups all over the world. Many of them continued their involvement with Tearfund as staff or consultants, and the lessons they had learnt from their successes – and failures – in the field helped to strengthen its expertise.

Tearfund's approach to using people in development was characteristically innovative. In 1971 it had provided financial support for agriculturists working for SAMS in Argentina, but it began to recognise the need to recruit and send its own personnel. The new system was kick-started by the appointment in 1973 of Ian Prior as Overseas Personnel Secretary and the creation of the Short Term Overseas Personnel – or STOP – programme. Ian recalled later:

Tearfund was supporting the work of the ACROSS consortium in southern Sudan, and various missionary societies involved in it were

looking to Tearfund to pay for people they were recruiting. But as time went by it was felt that Tearfund should play a more active role, not only being on the council of a consortium such as this but also actually recruiting workers.

Professionalism

66 We've always tried to learn from what we've done and apply it, so that we can try to do it better. Part of the passion, the motivation of serving God, has been to do the best job we possibly can, and through our years of work with our partners we have learnt things which are embedded in what we would nowadays call good practice.

But at the same time we don't want to be too cautious, because actually it's not just about us and our intellect and what we know, it's about God and where his Spirit is moving. We've got to be flexible and free enough to see where God is working with people.

Our work has become more professional, we have learnt to use our God-given experience and knowledge to greater effect, and that has been a good thing, but it always has to be held in balance. We don't want to become rigid and restrictive and miss that sense of where God might just happen to be working in a slightly different way than we are used to; we need to be open to that and free to follow it. 99

Ian Wallace, Tearfund 1996–2007

These were young, committed professionals who actually wanted to go with Tearfund rather than with a missionary society, and they also wanted to go for a specific term of two, three or four years. Although that was becoming more accepted by missionary societies in the 1970s, it was still a new thing for them to absorb into their operational policies, and so Tearfund became more of a specialist centre for short-term overseas personnel.

Once again Tearfund was catching a wave, particularly among younger Christians. Overseas locations were increasingly asking for short-term personnel, and more and more people were offering themselves for this kind of assignment. Tearfund was receiving on average half-a-dozen applications per week.

It began to advertise for the kind of people it was looking for: a drilling engineer for well-drilling in Ethiopia, a builder for hospitals and clinics in Burundi, a diesel mechanic to train nationals in Peru, an agriculturist for Bolivia, secondary school teachers for southern

1974: An advert for overseas service opportunities with Tearfund.

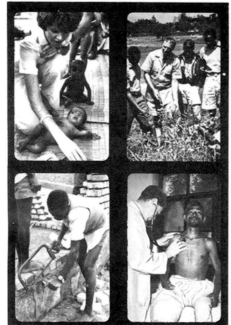

Will you go with your talents to a place of need in God's world?

TEAR Fund joins with the missionary societies and supports personnel for periods of service from nine months to three years in their STOP programme.

Are you prepared to commit yourself to a period overseas in the Thirld World?

Skilled people of all ages, who are committed Christians, are needed.

Doctors and nurses (in all fields of medicine)

Agriculturalists and carpenters

Engineers and builders

Administrators and secretaries . . . . and scores of others

TEAR Fund are in touch with the personnel needs of the missionary societies and are co-operating with them in placing and supporting qualified people in areas of the greatest need.

SHORT TERM OVERSEAS PERSONNEL

Sudan. And all these, of course, needed to be committed evangelical Christians. The people were going not just to do a job, but to build a bridge of relationship, and they needed to share the faith and values of those they were working with.

The essence of the STOP programme was to match roles with people. When people applied, Tearfund would seek God's purposes with them, as Ian explained:

> We would meet them and explore together whether God was at work in bringing them to Tearfund at this point. It would then be up to us as an organisation to discern whether there were skills here that God might want to use somewhere in the world. We would try to be in tune with that, to be flexible and to work at it to see if it was possible.

Over the following years, hundreds of Christian professionals went overseas with Tearfund. One of the first was Sue Mills, who was later to spend more than thirty years on the staff of Tearfund. In 1973 she was sent to Ethiopia:

Ethiopia, 1976: Tearfund overseas worker Sue Mills (left) at the SIM office in Guffra. Sue was sent to Ethiopia in 1973 to manage an orphanage but found herself involved in famine relief work. 'I realised that amidst incredible poverty people are still able to smile and have an amazing potential to give.'

It was the first time I had ever been out of the UK, and it was a terrific adventure. It dovetailed my Christian faith with something very, very practical and I was very excited, because this is what I had been looking for.

I only took a rucksack with me, and I had packed lots of sachets of Savlon because my mother was convinced I was going to die. They had all burst in transit, so my rucksack stank of disinfectant – I'm sure the people meeting me smelt me out rather than anything else.

Nepal, 1975: Physiotherapist Jennie Collins, Tearfund overseas worker, was based at the Shining Hospital, Pokhara. 'I learnt that however hard a situation is, actually change can happen if you stick with it and God intervenes.'

Sue had been recruited to manage an orphanage, but rapidly found herself pitched into helping people suffering from famine. In this and other sometimes harrowing assignments she found it was God who got her though:

I remember one time wandering around a refugee camp. I was tired and it was just horrible – rusty corrugated tin shacks and a quagmire of filth in between. I remember thinking, 'God, where are you? There is no way a loving God can be in this situation.' But then I saw a little girl, about three, totally naked, playing in this quagmire. She looked up shyly and then giggled, just pure merriment. I kind of felt God

saying, 'OK, she is surrounded by all you can see and certainly by all you can smell, but there is something inside her that is not touched by all that, and that is what I want you to work with. That's potential. Don't get overwhelmed by the scale, the enormity, by the fact that you can't change the world. Just put your eyes down on this little kiddie – that is what I want you to work with.'

In more recent years Tearfund has sent fewer specialists overseas, and their role has changed. Chartered surveyor and forester Steve Collins and his agriculturist wife Judith worked as environmental advisers with Tearfund's partner Mopawi in Honduras from 2001 to 2005. In earlier years, a key role of Tearfund overseas workers was to train a local person who could take over when they left, but that was not part of Steve and Judith's brief:

> Our role was more overall strengthening of the organisation, contributing research, advice on good practice, systems, etc, not training an individual to take our place. There's already so much expertise within partners, it's about recognising and building on their existing capacity rather than training somebody from scratch. It's focusing on

Cambodia, 2001: Like many others in countries ravaged by HIV and AIDS, Cambodian grandmother Yan struggled to look after her grandchildren after her daughter died because of AIDS. Channah, a volunteer from Tearfund's partner Servants to Asia's Urban Poor, supported the family. She herself had HIV and told Tearfund, 'Please pray for me because I want to carry on helping my patients. I still want towork hard for God until I die.'

the whole organisation and strengthening it rather than just on one person or group of people within it. I think there's a lot more sustainability in that, because what we were doing would stay with the organisation even if the people we were working with left.

The role has developed, but the motivation of working with a community to bring about change has remained the same. Like Sue Mills, Jennie Collins began a long association with Tearfund as an overseas worker. After a year in Bangladesh in the 1970s she spent a further seven in Nepal, and later joined Tearfund's staff, serving as International Director from 1992 to 2000. She then became once again a Tearfund overseas worker, as Executive Director of the United Mission to Nepal. Her experience has encapsulated something of Tearfund's vision in development, as she later reflected:

Empowering

With Tearfund, we don't do things *for* people. We empower them and we let them do it. That to me is very good.
Francis Mkandawire, General Secretary, Evangelical Association of Malawi

Why are we doing this? We are doing it to be part of the Kingdom that God is building, and to help people. People are changed. They say, 'We were in the dark, and now we are in the light; we had no power, but now we have power and know how to use it. We are still poor but we can solve our problems.' That is something of what God created people to be like. To me, that is the beginning of signs of the Kingdom. There is more to come, before Jesus comes again, but God is at work in those people's community and hearts and lives.

Those who are kind to the poor lend to the Lord, and he will reward them for what they have done. (Proverbs 19:17)

Listening

Across has been working in southern Sudan since 1972, and in all those years we've learnt that you need to be patient, you need to be doing things that are relevant and you need to be mindful of the people. They've gone through a lot of suffering and they need support so that they can regain their dignity as a people. The other lesson we've learnt is that whatever we do, we need to hear what they are saying. We don't just come with decisions, plans and programmes that have been made elsewhere: they may not be relevant. We need to scratch where it's itching, not scratch where it's not itching.
Anthony Poggo, Executive Director, Across, Sudan

Chapter 6

New Shoots

Tearfund's early success was due in no small measure to seizing opportunities when they presented themselves, with the faith-assured boldness that comes from believing that God is leading. It was innovative and spontaneous, taking what in retrospect might seem immoderate risks. On the face of it, sending a cheque for £10,000 to a theologically trained greengrocer in north-west London on the strength of a phone call and a meeting was just such a risk – but it's what got Tearcraft, literally, off the ground.

The greengrocer was Richard Adams, who'd gone into business importing fresh produce from developing countries because of his passion for trade justice. The phone call was in 1974, from Ian Prior, a university friend who was now working for Tearfund. Ian introduced Richard to Peter McNee, a Baptist missionary from New Zealand working in Bangladesh. Peter's work included helping people who had lost everything through war and natural disaster to earn a living by making and selling jute handicrafts. Tearfund had supported this work since 1972, when it paid for three women to be trained in jute weaving so that they could train others in their community.

Now he had come to the UK with craft samples from the Jute Works, a co-operative set up by church and development agencies in Dhaka, in the hope of finding a marketing outlet for them.

After meeting Peter, Richard decided to give it a try, and agreed to take delivery of half a ton of sikas (plant-bowl hangers), baskets, bags and mats. As he recalled later in his book *Who profits?* the New Zealander was taken aback, telling him,

> I thought you were mad, a greengrocer buying jute, but I certainly was not going to complain. I should know by now that God's world is full of surprises.

Where Tearcraft started: the Jute Works in Bangladesh, where women made sikas (plant-bowl hangers) and other products from jute.

The next surprise came in October of the same year, by which time Richard's stock had arrived and he had set up a mail order business to sell it with Ray Skinner, another university friend who was now a curate in Newcastle upon Tyne. It was a further call from Ian Prior, this time inviting Richard to a meeting at Tearfund with George Hoffman, who had visited Peter McNee and the craft workers in Bangladesh. They met the next day, and George outlined his idea: Tearfund was sending a plane with relief supplies to Bangladesh, which would return empty. How about filling it with craft products for the return flight? And would Richard fly out to organise it?

Richard agreed, and estimated that the cost of a planeload of handicrafts would be £10,000. The next day a cheque for that amount arrived from Tearfund, and on 12 November 1974 he flew to Bangladesh.

When the plane returned packed with handicrafts, everything was

Tearcraft: the first steps

❝ Three years ago TEAR Fund enabled three women from the village of Chandpur to go to Dacca for training in jute weaving. Those women returned to their own community and that was the start of the transformation. First a group of fifty-five beggars stopped begging and began to work with the new jute co-operative. Within a year they were earning £297 per month. Soon they had a joint bank account with a deposit of £178. Peter McNee, the missionary leader who pioneered this programme, wrote, 'The children were no longer on the streets, they were in school. Their broken-down houses had been repaired, they were eating three meals a day, and the only relief I gave them was about 9p worth of raw jute with which to begin the whole work.' ❞
From Tearfund's Annual Report, 1974/5

in place for a full-scale business operation, financed by Tearfund and managed by Richard Adams. Two days before Christmas 1974 Tearcraft was registered as a trading name. Tony Neeves was responsible for promoting the new business:

One Saturday my wife and I photographed the first Tearcraft catalogue. She was the model and didn't want her face in the photographs, so everything was neck down. I remember the catalogue was a little A5

Sri Lanka, 1978: At Gospel House Handicrafts, young unemployed men from poor areas of the capital, Colombo, are given work and dignity. The products they make are sold by Tearcraft.

The first Tearcraft catalogue, produced in 1975.

thing, brown in colour. Tearcraft just took off – it was a tremendously exciting development.

The first Tearcraft catalogue was mailed to Tearfund supporters in February 1975. It boasted just forty-six items, of which fifteen were jute sikas and the rest a collection of jute bags and table mats, cane baskets, coconut shell jewellery and stuffed toys. You could have bought one of everything and still have change from £50 – including postage and packing.

Sales grew rapidly: by January 1976 Tearcraft had sold more than £100,000 worth of products. The third catalogue, in autumn 1976,

In 1984 Cliff Richard took to London's Oxford Street to promote a Tearcraft sale.

TEAR FUND ANNOUNCES
TEAR CRAFT

"I wish you could see the difference between those who have purposeful work and those who have nothing to do. The restoration of dignity and self-respect is remarkable." (Rev Peter McNee, Co-operative Leader, Chandpur, Bangladesh.)

Tear Craft has been set up by TEAR Fund to market handicrafts from developing countries. Already in Bangladesh some 30 co-operatives have been formed and over 3,000 women trained to use their traditional skills in producing goods, mainly from jute and local raw materials.

Handicrafts are labour intensive, produce valuable foreign exchange, and enable people in the destructive grip of poverty to build hope for the future.

There is extensive Christian involvement at every level of the project, and with minimum administration costs the village workers obtain a maximum profit.

These goods are sold mainly through mail order. Just fill in the coupon to receive the attractive free catalogue with over forty items for you to choose from.

Remember, every pound's worth of goods sold means money earned to buy food for a whole family.

Please send me one copy of the TEAR Craft catalogue.

Name

Address

Post to: Tear Craft, 1 Bridgeman Road, Teddington, Middlesex TW11 9AJ.

1975: Tearfund advertises its new venture to market handicrafts from developing countries in the UK.

Kath Shortley learns about batik on a visit to Intermission, India, in 2005. When U Benjamin and his wife Parwin felt God was calling them to help orphans and street children, they set up the Intermission training centre in Chennai, enabling teenage girls to learn batik, weaving and sewing.

took sales to £180,000 with products from seven countries, and the next year they doubled again, to £380,000.

The business was booming under Richard Adams' direction, but he found himself increasingly at odds with Tearfund over its commitment to purchasing goods only from groups organised by or associated with evangelical Christians. In 1979 he left, and with financial support from Tearfund set up Traidcraft, which over the next quarter-century grew to become a leader in the fair trade movement, whose products are often sold alongside Tearcraft by Tearfund volunteers.

From the beginning, volunteers were vital in the success of Tearcraft. The new idea caught the imagination of Tearfund supporters, and by 1977 there were more than fifty voluntary representatives registered to sell the crafts in different parts of the country. One of

Being fair

❝ I didn't hear about fair trade from anybody. I read my Bible and I learnt that I am to love and be fair to my brothers and sisters. I think that fair trade is the best example of this. ❞

Yannina Meza de Rietveld, who set up Peruvian craft producer Manos Amigas with her brother in 1991. Manos Amigas, whose products are sold through Tearcraft, provides work for groups of local artisans, and profits are used to support church-based education and feeding programmes for children in slum areas of the capital, Lima.

them, Kath Shortley, ordered £200 of jute products to sell. The venture got off to a shaky start:

> We were going to display the stock at a special church service, but unfortunately it didn't arrive in time. So we thought, oh my goodness, what are we going to do with this? My husband opened the box, looked into it and said, 'Well, what you've got here is £200 worth of string! I hope you think you're going to sell this.'
>
> I did, and continued selling, and gradually it got to the point where the house was just overtaken by this stuff. It would be time to go to bed and it still wasn't clear, and we'd have to clear it off onto the floor.

South Africa, 2005: Tearcraft partner Umtha was providing jobs for forty disadvantaged Xhosa women, including Christine Manyonya (pictured right). Umtha (which means 'ray of light') is a jewellery-making business that aims to help local people overcome poverty and deprivation.

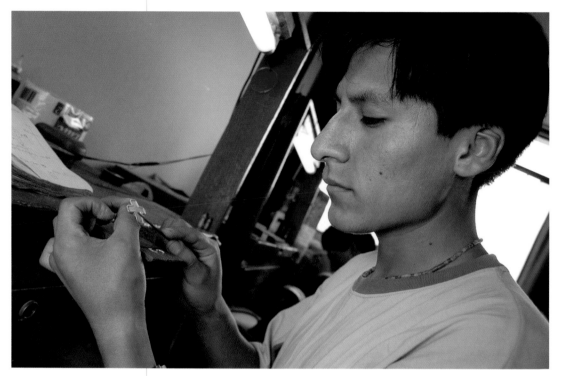

Peru, 2004: Freddie Rivas, a craftworker in Lima, making jewellery for Tearcraft partner Manos Amigas. Since 1975 Tearcraft has provided job opportunities, fair wages and safe working environments for thousands of craftworkers around the world. Freddie told Tearfund, 'It's very emotional to see my jewellery worn. I'm proud that people outside my country value the things I've made.'

Eventually we opened a shop selling Tearcraft and ran it for twenty-seven years, and the thing was, it actually sold really well.

Three decades later, Tearcraft had a national network of more than 1,100 volunteers selling its products – some of them selling more than £20,000 worth a year. Like many others, Kath was still heavily involved in Tearcraft:

It was a big risk for Tearfund at the beginning, but I'm sure God was behind it, and I'm sure it was one of the first moves that brought fair trade into being. We've seen divine intervention, because the market-place has been so difficult, the hurdles have been so big. I'm convinced beyond a shadow of a doubt that it was the Lord's work and he chose Tearfund to do it.

I never cease to be amazed at the hours, the time, the energy and the passion that people have for Tearcraft and fair trade.

By the time Tearcraft celebrated its thirtieth birthday, its annual sales were approaching £2 million, with a catalogue containing more than 350 products. It was working with nineteen producer groups in ten countries, in a partnership that enabled hundreds of people to work with dignity and purpose and to provide for themselves and their families.

Another Tearfund initiative with early links to Bangladesh was its long-running involvement in child sponsorship. When Jennie Evans flew on the Tearfund relief plane to Bangladesh in 1974, her fellow passenger was Sally Lambert, who had joined Tearfund earlier that

Tearcraft: work with dignity

Sri Lankan John Karunaratne was in his mid-forties when he became a Christian. He gave up his job to become an evangelist, and having seen so many unemployed young men around the capital, Colombo, he began to dream of providing them with work. When a local pastor gave him an old spin-dryer, John used the motor to make a lathe, and in 1976 a business came into being: Gospel House Handicrafts. Tearcraft heard of the project and placed an order for its simple wooden products. Today the business makes wooden toys and other craft goods, exporting to Europe and North America, giving employment to forty-five artisans and creating work for dozens more in the locality. Since John's death the business has been run by his widow and sons, winning numerous awards for innovation and business success.

"WHOEVER WELCOMES IN MY NAME ONE SUCH CHILD AS THIS, WELCOMES ME."

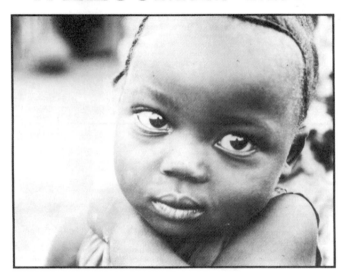

These well known words of Jesus are at the heart of Tear Fund's Childcare Programme. They have brought health-care and education, food and clothing to more than 4,000 children in Asia and Latin America. But more. This link has shown that someone, somewhere, loves them, cares for them, and prays that each one of them will come to know that fulness of life that Jesus offers to them

This link of love is provided through our Sponsorship Programme. Complete the application form below today, it will help you to discover how to welcome "one such child as this" in His name.

I would like to sponsor a needy child through the Tear Fund Childcare Programme.

Please select the child who needs me the most ☐ I would prefer a girl ☐ a boy. ☐

TEAR FUND

I would prefer to pay by ☐ Banker's order*

☐ monthly £8   ☐ Cheque (made payable to Tear Fund)

☐ ¼year £24

☐ Annual £96   ☐ Under Deed of Covenant*

* Details will be sent

Name(s) _____
BLOCK LETTERS PLEASE

Address _____
_____
_____

For Group Sponsorship: please state name of Group.

Post to: Childcare Department, Tear Fund, 11 Station Road, Teddington, Middlesex TW11 9AJ.

Printed in England by Gaffyne and Brown, Teddington.

year and was in charge of the programme. It had been launched in June of that year as the Tearfund 'Family Plan'.

Sponsors donated £5 per month, with which a needy child in Bangladesh or India would be fed, clothed, housed and educated. Tearfund planned to arrange 1,800 sponsorships in the first year. Keen to ensure that child sponsorship did not grow out of proportion to the organisation's existing priorities, it intended that the donations should not exceed one-fifth of its overall income.

Within weeks of the scheme being announced, Tearfund had received more than 500 letters from individuals, families, groups and churches asking for more information. Before any literature had been produced, nearly 100 children had been assigned sponsors willing to support them financially and in prayer for at least a year.

The new initiative was the outcome of two years of discussion with World Vision International, which already had an extensive child sponsorship programme, and was launched in conjunction with World Vision Canada. By 1975, however, Tearfund was looking for a change of direction. The original scheme was supporting children living in orphanages, and this kind of institutional care was coming under criticism from childcare experts. Moreover, the

Opposite: An advert for Tearfund's Childcare Programme in 1978.

Haiti, 1996: Dina Ymbert, 13, lived with her parents and six brothers and sisters in the village of Hostin. The family was poor, but Dina was able to go to school thanks to being sponsored through Tearfund's Partners in Childcare programme.

management of the homes was not always in the hands of evangelical Christians, which conflicted with Tearfund's basic values. This, combined with a shortage of children to sponsor, led Tearfund to consider switching its partnership to Compassion International, a US-based evangelical organisation with a worldwide child sponsorship programme that put a more direct focus on helping the child through the family and the local church rather than through institutional care.

> **I**s not this the kind of fasting I have chosen: to loose the chains of injustice and untie the cords of the yoke, to set the oppressed free and break every yoke? Is it not to share your food with the hungry and to provide the poor wanderer with shelter – when you see the naked, to clothe them, and not to turn away from your own flesh and blood? (Isaiah 58:6–7)

The change was made, and over the next twenty-four years the two organisations enabled Christians in the UK and Ireland to sponsor children in developing countries.

Most children in the programme entered as they started school at the age of five or six and didn't leave until they were eighteen or nineteen, after which they received vocational training to help them fend for themselves. The approach was to support the child within the context of the family, school, church and community, and to be holistic – addressing social and political factors of poverty, alongside health, educational and environmental issues, not just economic welfare. All of this was within a strong Christian context: as Compassion's Wess Stafford said in 1986,

> In every aspect of our programme we ask ourselves, 'What does the child need in order not only to survive but to become the fulfilled adult God intends him to be?'

Child sponsorship, like Tearcraft, was a way to engage people with the issues of poverty and development, perhaps for the first time. Many people sponsored a child, for example, because they wanted their own children to learn something about poverty and grow up to be sympathetic and compassionate people.

Carole Allen joined Tearfund in 1980 and was in charge of the childcare team for fifteen years until she retired in 2004:

> I felt it was a very positive thing, because we were having some impact on these lives, helping children in poor places to reach their potential. Many of the sponsors told me how much they'd gained from it too –

their own children were learning a lot, gaining a deeper understanding of the situation children in other countries were living in.

To the supporter it offered something achievable – it was promoted under the appealing slogan, 'No one person can change the world. But I can help change the world for one person.' For Tearfund, it was effective in attracting committed supporters who would develop a long-term relationship with the organisation.

The scheme, later renamed 'Partners in Childcare', grew steadily: by 1976 there were 1,300 children being sponsored at £6 per month,

Transform

❝ When we go on Transform to live, eat, work, talk, play, laugh, cry with people who have been marginalised – people who have become statistics on our televisions – God walks with us in an intimate way. He allows us to see the world from his perspective, he strips away the clutter of our culture and he reorders us into what he intended us to be. ❞

Sue Towler, Tearfund 2002–

Uganda, 2005: Rebels of the Lord's Resistance Army in northern Uganda sowed fear by kidnapping children and forcing them into killings and sex-slavery. As a result, thousands of children and women were forced to become 'night commuters', walking in from their villages every night to seek safety in the towns. Supporters of the Children at Risk programme helped Tearfund's partner Noah's Ark to provide a safe shelter for 3,000 children every night in Gulu.

and five years later the total was 11,000 – by this time at £10 per month. By 1999 the number of children in the sponsorship programme was more than 28,000. As the scheme expanded, a number of related specialised giving programmes were launched, for work with refugees, meals sponsorship for children, food-related projects, vocational training, and development programmes in particular countries.

In 1999, however, Tearfund ended its childcare programme, believing that the time had come for a change. Graham Fairbairn, who as Home Director in the 1990s had overseen the programme, explained:

> There had been a long debate in Tearfund about whether child sponsorship was good development or not. Our sister organisation TEAR Australia was unhappy about child sponsorship, and many of the development specialists in Tearfund shared that view. We could see that to run a sponsorship programme you needed stable situations. If the economic or political situation became volatile, the programmes had to be closed down. There were positive aspects to child sponsorship, and many of the children found faith in Christ, but its individual emphasis didn't fit with our growing vision for bringing change to

Colombia, 2003: Lisbeth, Gustavo and Joana were teenagers with one thing in common – their fathers had all been brutally murdered in the country's merciless civil conflict. Tearfund's partners were helping hundreds of children come to terms with their traumatic experiences, with support from the Children at Risk programme.

the community. We wanted to do something for children at risk who were being reached through our partners' development work.

Following the decision, Compassion International opened a UK operation. Tearfund ceased its own promotion of child sponsorship, recommending Compassion to people who wanted to become sponsors, and instead launched a new 'Children at Risk' programme. This focused on children who fell outside the scope of traditional sponsorship programmes. Instead of sponsoring an individual child, Tearfund supporters were encouraged to give to help children whose needs and rights were not being met because of poverty, exploitation, abuse, disability, conflict and discrimination. By 2007, 'Children at Risk' donors were supporting 119 projects in 44 countries.

While child sponsorship came to an end, Tearfund remained committed to the wider goal of creating a relationship between its

France, 1971: Volunteers on one of Tearfund's first summer work camps built a chapel in Vendôme. One participant's feedback was: 'A suggestion for future work camps: make sure everyone goes out expecting to work, to get dirty, blistered hands, and a bent, aching back.' The camps were a success, but lacked a 'relief' element, so the following year's camp had a more needy location: the Nazareth Hospital.

supporters and the people in poorer communities that they were helping – a goal which it had pursued since its foundation. Born in an age when international travel was beginning to come within the grasp of ordinary people, Tearfund made it possible for people not just to read about poverty and give money, but to see it with their own eyes and make their own practical contribution. At first, the horizons were fairly limited: in 1970 and 1971, summer work camps for volunteers aged eighteen to twenty-five were organised in France, Austria and Germany. Expectations were somewhat limited too, albeit very much in the spirit of the time: as *Tear Times* announced in 1971, 'Although the need is mostly for men to undertake various manual jobs in building construction or renovation, there are some opportunities for female help.'

In 1972 the programme ventured outside Europe: two teams of twenty-one volunteers went to the Nazareth Hospital in Israel to help with building maintenance and its day-to-day running. The men constructed a lift shaft, laid oxygen and water pipes, and insulated and cemented roofs, while, as *Tear Times* put it, 'the girls undertook mainly domestic work, on the wards, in the kitchen, laundry and sewing room'. In later years, of course, female members of the teams would play an equal part in the tasks, lending their hands to

Tearfund's Task Force Teams enabled people to go and experience life in a poor community – and do something useful while they were there. Practical work combined with learning from Tearfund's partners made it a life-changing experience for many.

First hand experience

It was a visit to Uganda that opened Fiona Morrison's eyes to what the world is really like. In 1994, while a student at Aberdeen University, she went with a Tearfund Task Force Team to work for two months at the Church of Uganda hospital in Kisiizi:

'I got the shock of my life. We arrived in the middle of a malaria epidemic. The hospital had just over 100 beds, but more than 300 patients. People were lying on the floors and sleeping on mats in the grounds. Growing up in the church I was used to hearing about these things, but to actually be there and see it was just incredible.

'At times we felt like guilty spectators: what's the use of being here? But when we tried to apologise for being in the way, the people at the hospital didn't see us like that at all. They were absolutely delighted that we were there. They said they viewed us as a gift from God, that we'd come to help them.

'We spent a couple of weeks painting a new tuberculosis ward but we were still thinking, what have we really done? But then a man from UNICEF visited, and when he saw that the ward had been painted and made ready, he committed to giving the hospital the rest of the funding needed to get it open and operational. The hospital said to us, "You've done an amazing thing. We didn't have anyone to paint, and if you hadn't been here and painted it he would have said we were nowhere near ready and we wouldn't have had that money." They were so happy about that, and we started to feel that maybe we had made a difference after all.'

bricklaying and other traditionally 'male' skills in ways that might have seemed quite unorthodox in the 1970s.

Between 1970 and 1985 more than 500 young people took part in summer work teams in fifteen countries, typically involving building and renovation, working in health and rural development programmes and helping to lead youth camps. 'They come back with a new understanding of the needs and challenges of the developing world, and many of them eventually return overseas with Tear Fund or with other missions,' wrote David Applin, Overseas Personnel Director, in 1986.

In that year the work was expanded. The first step was to change the name to 'Task Force Teams' and to send teams at different times of the year, not just in the summer holidays, as well as widening the age range from the twenty- to twenty-five-year-olds taking part up to then. The stated aim of these teams was threefold: to complete a useful piece of work, to bring encouragement to the local Christian community, and to challenge team members as to their Christian vocation.

The Transform
programme enabled
volunteers to spend from
two weeks to four months
in a Tearfund-supported
project, working hard –
and making new friends.

Later that year, teams were reported at work in seven countries:
Jordan (maintenance and repair work at a school for the deaf),
Poland (extending church premises to provide facilities for the com-
munity), Ghana (construction work at a Bible college), Zaire (helping
local masons build two staff houses at the Evangelical Medical
Centre in Nyankunde), Kenya (repairing a water system at Lake
Naivasha), Uganda (repairing and improving equipment and build-
ings at Kisiizi Hospital) and Tanzania (redecorating buildings at
Kilimatinde Hospital). Teams were also sent to urban centres in the UK.

By 2007 the Transform programme was sending up to 500 people
each year to work with Tearfund partners in more than twenty countries. As David Westlake, Tearfund's Youth Director from 1996, noted,

It's not so much about them going overseas to change the world – although we hope they will be a blessing – but more a huge opportunity to expose mainly young team members to people who are working out their Christianity in very difficult circumstances. It's about them coming back ruined for the western dream but absolutely committed to the dream of the Kingdom of God.

For David, providing an opportunity to engage with poverty at first hand, in a practical way, has been an important part of Tearfund's work with young people:

God's heart for justice is written all the way through the Bible but it has not always been a strong emphasis in discipleship in the UK. We wanted to put before young Christians an alternative understanding of discipleship, a way of living which is wholeheartedly committed to the Lordship of Christ, to worship, to prayer, to Bible study and to personal evangelism, but which also puts a focus on the needs of those who are put down.

In recent years God has been stirring up lots of churches to think about justice issues, so in some ways I have felt I was pushing against an open door – a door that had been opened by years of work by Tearfund, by John Stott and by so many other people. People were intellectually convinced that concern for the poor needed to be an integral part of their faith. They just didn't know what to do, so the challenge was to give them some very practical ways to outwork that conviction.

Youth

❝ It's a huge privilege to meet young people and discover that something we've written or said has become a lens for them through which they've suddenly understood Christianity – it all made sense and their whole lives became aflame with faith and love and action. To be involved in their faith journey like that is phenomenal, and to have some of them end up working for us is even more exciting. The fact that these people are carrying this flame for justice and will ignite other people is actually what it's all about. ❞

David Westlake, Tearfund 1996–

Terry Tearaway

For generations of children in the 1980s and 1990s Terry Tearaway was the face of Tearfund. He made his first appearance in 1979, when Youth Secretary John Eames launched the Tearaways club for Tearfund's young supporters. He appeared first in occasional letters but his identity and character became more firmly established in 1980, when the regular free publication *Tearaways* replaced the earlier *Roundabout*. Cartoon strips featuring Terry, first in black and white and then in colour – and later his feisty sister Tina – introduced children to poverty in the developing world.

Terry Tearaway went on to appear in videos, although in his first animated appearance he had to present the whole programme from his bed, because the budget would only extend as far as head and arms. He travelled the world, reporting for Tearfund, and when David Adeney resigned as chief executive of Tearfund he applied for the job, but was not shortlisted. He eventually retired from Tearfund in 1997. Among his other distinctions was appearing in an early computer game, *Terry on the move*, developed by RE teacher John Fewings and released in 1985.

Terry Gibson, who directed Terry's videos, remembers: 'Unlike us adults, Terry could hang around with kids in a place like the slums of Cairo and be on equal terms with them. He had the ability to see situations through completely unprejudiced eyes, which was significant for anyone watching.'

Fiona Morrison is one of thousands who have been overseas with Tearfund and found the experience has changed their life. In 1994, when a student at Aberdeen University, she went with a Task Force Team to work for two months at the Church of Uganda hospital in Kisiizi:

> We were helping to build an extension to the local primary school and painting new hospital wards, and travelled to outlying districts with hospital staff providing healthcare for new mothers. It was my first real encounter with Tearfund and it was amazing.
>
> I'd been brought up in the evangelical wing of the church, but it frustrated me that while there was such an emphasis on scripture and preaching, I didn't find the same emphasis on social action, on actually trying to do practical things in the world. But in Tearfund I really found what I was looking for. It showed me for the first time that it's possible to do both. The Task Force Team gave me an awareness that it's possible to preach the word and still be Christ's hands and feet in this world.
>
> The vision of the people at the hospital was the same as Tearfund's. There was no difference between having your Christian faith – they were so openly evangelical, and the hospital ran a couple of huge mission events while we there – and doing the social action, getting stuck in where people were in need. If practical help was needed somewhere you did it, because that was the fulfilment of your Christian faith. There was no agonising over it – am I emphasising one at the expense of the other? It was just part and parcel of the way of life: you preached your faith and you walked and lived your faith as well.

Uganda, 1994: Tearfund Transform team members Fiona Morrison and David Young hard at work at Kisiizi hospital.

Many people who went on overseas teams came back wanting to use their time for Tearfund, and joined its volunteer network. This is what Fiona did – in 2003 she became a volunteer speaker for Tearfund, speaking on average once a month to churches and groups and local media about her

experiences and Tearfund's work. She's passionate about poverty, and her experience of life in a poorer part of the world has given her a lasting motivation to work for change:

> I live in a country where I don't want for anything and I'm so aware that so many people don't. I feel helpless a lot of the time, but working with Tearfund I feel maybe I am helping to make a difference. I think I've seen too much to do nothing. I can't do nothing, knowing what I know.
>
> Doing what I can for Tearfund helps me really feel that I'm living my faith as fully as possible – I'm not just saying this is what I believe, I can do something practical as well. I've got a very, very high opinion of Tearfund, and it's made a huge difference to my life, giving me an awareness of the world and an outlet for doing something about it as well.

Tearfund attracted the support of volunteers from the very beginning, and they rapidly became an indispensable part of its work. Within a few years of it starting, the increasing number of requests for Tearfund speakers was putting an impossible load on the small office team, and it was hoped area representatives could help share that load. The first conference to inform, equip and encourage local representatives was held on a weekend in November 1974, with about sixty people attending. The aim was to bring the representatives into a closer working and praying relationship with Tearfund.

'Because the poor are plundered and the needy groan, I will now arise,' says the Lord. 'I will protect them from those who malign them.' (Psalm 12:5)

Graham Fairbairn joined Tearfund's staff as Regional Organiser for Ireland in 1979, but had been a voluntary area representative since 1977:

> The volunteer programme was completely new. I didn't know of any other organisation that was running anything as sophisticated as this. The volunteers were given training and a job description, and there were different categories of representatives.
>
> It was a real step forward in getting Tearfund earthed in the churches, and having representatives in the churches really cemented Tearfund's relationship with them.

Since then the network has grown to some 4,000 volunteers engaged in a variety of roles – representing Tearfund in their church, speaking about Tearfund, leading a prayer group, promoting campaigning activities, helping at events, raising awareness of Tearfund in the local media, and others. For Paul Brigham, Tearfund's UK Director, Church and Supporter Relations, these volunteers make Tearfund unique in the world of relief and development:

> We serve a relational God, and all Scripture points to the fact that he works through relationships. He is more concerned about who we are than about what we do. If Tearfund is going to build anything it has to be through relationships, and our volunteers take that relationship into the local church. People's experience of who Tearfund is, ultimately, is that volunteer in their church who stands up and asks for prayer or asks them to give or to back a campaign.

Mixed in with the joy and excitement of a growing, ground-breaking organisation there were times of pain. Tearfund water engineer Andy Meakins, who had worked in Ethiopia for nearly twenty years, was killed when his hijacked airliner crashed in the Indian Ocean in

Tearfund nurse Heather Sinclair (centre) was released in August 1987 after being held by rebels in southern Sudan. She told reporters, 'I was never really frightened because of my strong Christian faith and because I knew that God had called me to Sudan.'

Tearfund water engineer Andy Meakins at work with Ethiopian villagers.

November 1996. In 1999, relief workers Nick Evens and Kevin Lay died in a plane crash on their way to join Tearfund's team helping refugees rebuild their homes in Kosovo. In later years, as Tearfund expanded its emergency relief operations in dangerous areas, locally recruited workers lost their lives in violent incidents: surveyor Maheshe Chishagala Evariste was shot by rebels in the Democratic Republic of Congo in 2003, and Rashid Mohamed Adam was killed by a mob while working as a driver in Darfur in 2006. More happily, there was relief when Tearfund nurse Heather Sinclair, who had been kidnapped by rebels in southern Sudan in July 1987, was released after forty-nine days in captivity.

A difficult time for the organisation as a whole came in the late 1980s, when Tearfund parted company with George Hoffman. A visionary and entrepreneurial leader, he was described by Gilbert Kirby, General Secretary of the EA from 1955 to 1966, as 'God's man to get Tearfund off the ground'. He brought to Tearfund a passion and a gift in communication that put the infant organisation on the map, and his lean looks and mobile face led Anglican evangelical leader Michael Saward to call him 'the best visual aid for Tearfund'. As John Capon, editor of *Tear Times* in the 1980s, put it, his chief assets in building Tearfund were 'his face, his voice and his pen'. Tony Neeves later recalled:

> George was an utterly amazing man and I can see why God chose him to start Tearfund and lead it. He was a remarkably exciting visionary who inspired loyalty and passion.

Visionaries, of course, are not always easy to live and work with, and George himself acknowledged that he had a tendency to 'impetuous decisions, taken without having thought through all the implications' and to 'carry people with my own enthusiasm when they're not ready to embark upon something'.

Under his leadership Tearfund saw rapid and substantial growth, in income, personnel, operations and impact. By the late 1980s, however, a number of tensions were developing. Today it would be described as a case of 'founder's syndrome', when the organisation becomes too big to be led by the charismatic personality and vision of its founding chief executive alone, too complex for one person to control every aspect of its operation. The very qualities that helped get it off the ground become a barrier to further healthy growth, and a change in leadership style is required.

GHACOE was born out of the Ghana Congress on Evangelism in 1977 and was for many years a Tearfund partner. With a vision to reach Ghana's women with the gospel and encourage them in Christian discipleship, it taught women income-boosting and agricultural skills.

Guinea, 1997: Tearfund's partner SECADOS distributes cooking oil to refugees in Nongoa camp. Emmanuel Kourouma of SECADOS said, 'Before you tell somebody that you have faith, you have to show it through your actions.'

In Tearfund's case this led to a painful period which was resolved finally in 1988, when the board terminated his employment. By the grace of God, however, the organisation that he had led moved into its next stage of growth. It could have been a mortal blow to Tearfund, but just as God seems to have had his hand on it throughout its history, so it survived. As John Harvey later recalled,

> There was concern that the whole thing could fall apart, but in fact it just carried on without a blip in either its income or its activities.

The next chief executive was David Adeney, who had joined Tearfund in December 1986 as Operational Director, responsible for its day-to-day running after a successful career in senior management in the business world. David brought the stability and planned development that the organisation needed for the next stage of its growth:

> It wasn't easy for Tearfund to go through a leadership change, because George was so much a figurehead of the work when he left. But the Lord gave us stability. I was Acting General Director for a while, and

then the board decided I should continue to lead the organisation. I'd always looked up to Tearfund as an exciting expression of Christian activity, but I knew it needed to strengthen its management systems.

Under his leadership, Tearfund focused on becoming more professional. Internally, this meant developing structures and systems appropriate to an organisation of its size, while externally it meant creating a new level of professionalism in Tearfund's relief and development work. Ian Wallace recalled:

> This was the time when Tearfund began to come out of the evangelical ghetto. We began to engage more with other agencies and bodies, especially in disaster response. At the same time, the development world was beginning to realise that the 1980s idea of values-free development was a myth, and the pendulum was swinging back in favour of values-informed development, which was what we were doing.
>
> As we've grown in confidence, we've realised that we don't have to hide who we are in order to do development work. If you keep yourself in the ghetto, you reinforce the perception that you have a hidden agenda. But if you are open and honest, people come to understand and respect who you are, even if they don't completely agree with you.

All they asked was that we should continue to remember the poor, the very thing I had been eager to do all along. (Galatians 2:10)

A scene from Tearfund's 1994 youth video *Illegal Access*. Shot on a shoestring budget, it used Birmingham drama students for the main parts – including as male lead a young Jimi Mistry (left), who nine years later was the star of Hollywood movie *The Guru*.

Ethiopia, 2003: For Hebiso Untasi, 60, teff seed provided by Tearfund's partner the Kale Heywet Church made the difference between hunger and plenty. The crop would provide seed for his ten children and five grandchildren. The Kale Heywet Church was founded by missionaries and grew rapidly under indigenous leadership: by 2007 it had more than 5 million active members in 5,749 local churches. The church was involved in a wide range of relief and development programmes and had a long-standing partnership with Tearfund.

We've discovered that we can learn a lot from other people working in this sector, and at the same time there's a lot they can learn from us, as long as we have the right attitude of humility and openness. This is part of our witness as Christians.

Bill Crooks observed the impact of this change:

In the 1990s Tearfund started to put its head above the parapet and realise it could make relationships with other groups and learn, which set it up for the period from about 2000 onwards when it became quite a major player in the development community in Britain. Advocacy put us on the map in lots of ways, but also in areas such as AIDS and disaster preparedness we were getting ourselves a lot more into working groups and forums where the name Tearfund was known. Tearfund got out and started networking and learning and being part of other groups. I suppose Tearfund just got braver about being part of that wider world.

By the time David Adeney left, Tearfund had gained the confidence to say it could do a professional job, recognised by government and peer bodies alike, without losing its committed Christian identity. For David himself, however, something else stood out during his time at the helm of Tearfund:

> If I look back over my time in Tearfund and point to anything which really stirred me and which I'm pleased we began to do something about, it's AIDS. It was very controversial because in those days in North America in particular it was regarded as a disease of homosexuals. Some people in the evangelical world wouldn't have anything to do with it. I remember quite strong debates about whether we should take a proactive stance with our partners and ask how we could help, and I'm very pleased that we did. We linked up with ACET, and HIV and AIDS began to be an important part of our work.

After nine years with the organisation, David Adeney felt he had done what God had brought him to Tearfund for, and announced his resignation. During that time, Tearfund's income and expenditure had doubled, its staff numbers had grown by 50 per cent, and it had become the country's fifth largest relief and development agency.

On his departure, once again, God provided the person the

Prayer

Prayer is part of the day-to-day life of Tearfund's staff and its partners around the world, and Tearfund recognises the enormous role that the prayer of its supporters plays. Tearfund prayer groups meet in different parts of the UK and Ireland, and the organisation provides prayer resources for its supporters. For many years it sent out a quarterly prayer diary with *Tear Times*, and in 1974 it started distributing prayer cassettes to people who wanted to pray. In 1992 Tearfund introduced *World Watch Prayer Link*, a monthly bulletin to enable informed prayer for critical international situations, which later became a weekly email service. In 2007 Tearfund launched its new vision, at the heart of which was a focus on prayer.

organisation needed. Doug Balfour, a younger man with a background in business management and overseas relief work, joined in October 1995 and launched a radical shake-up of the organisation, restructuring it in order to position it for strategic growth into the beginning of the twenty-first century. Like David Adeney, he served for nine years; under Doug's leadership too Tearfund's income doubled again, and the organisation expanded significantly in the scope of its operations and impact.

In 2004 Doug left Tearfund to lead Global Alliance (later Integral), a network of thirteen Christian development and relief agencies

Bangladesh, 2002: The small business loans of Tearfund partner HEED enabled poor women to start keeping chickens – adding to their family income and increasing their standing in the community.

around the world enabling joint responses to disasters and long-term poverty. Graham Fairbairn recalled:

> Doug brought us a sense of energy, of direction, of strategic planning. He enabled us to work out very clearly where we wanted to get to, and to be specific about growth for a purpose, growth that would deliver the vision. He also made the whole thing much more participatory than anything we'd known before – everyone was involved in contributing to the vision, which was then consolidated and shaped into a ten-year strategy.

In 2005 the baton of leadership passed to Matthew Frost, a successful business director and management consultant who had also worked on relief programmes in Afghanistan and the Horn of Africa. Like his predecessors, Matthew brought to Tearfund the gifts and experience needed to give the by now major organisation a clear strategic focus for the next phase of its life.

Since its inception Tearfund has had only four chief executives. Graham Fairbairn worked in senior positions with all four of them:

> I feel that each of them was right for the time. George, David, Doug and Matthew – each has been exactly what Tearfund needed. It's as if at each point in Tearfund's evolution God brought the right person with the right qualities to lead it on to its next phase of growth and development. I see that as part of the grace of God upon Tearfund.

When the South Asia tsunami struck in December 2004, Tearfund supporters gave £8.6 million. This enabled Tearfund and its partners not just to meet immediate needs with emergency relief supplies, but also to help devastated communities put their lives back together. Here homes are being rebuilt for 300 families in Banda Aceh, Indonesia, with Tearfund support.

Cry to God

❝ Jesus cried over Jerusalem, but then went down to give up his life there. As followers of Jesus we should allow ourselves to cry aloud and to God for our cities. Then be ready to go, directed by God, to live and speak his message of love and hope. ❞

Andy Meakins, Tearfund, 1995

Part of God's blessing on Tearfund has been the steady increase in its income. There have been only three years when the income has fallen, and in both cases it recovered with a rise the following year. By 2003/04 it had reached £35.2 million, and then the extraordinarily generous response of supporters to the Indian Ocean tsunami of Boxing Day 2004 and to the suffering of displaced people in Darfur, Sudan, sent it soaring to more than £52 million in 2004/05. There would have been good grounds for thinking that this was an aberration, a temporary upsurge because of the horror of the tsunami, but remarkably the following year it stayed at the same level – and all this with fundraising costs running at just 8p in the pound.

By 2006 Tearfund was working with 297 partners in a total of 565 projects around the world. Echoing John Stott's booklet *Walk in his shoes* of thirty years before, Matthew Frost's message to supporters reinforced Tearfund's continuing vision:

> The local church, here and overseas, is the organisation Tearfund works through. Nothing is as effective as a catalyst for mobilising people to deliver practical help and lasting hope.
>
> And it's when the church serves the poor that it fulfils its whole calling. Matthew 25 drives home the importance of responding to 'the least' – not as a fringe activity but an essential part of living out our faith.
>
> This unambiguous call has driven our work this year. And you've responded by giving, praying and campaigning. You've stood alongside those caught in poverty's grip. You've enabled our church-based partners to continue their work with local communities.
>
> I'm convinced that our mission, individually and as members of local churches, must be integral to all we do. Our generosity, simplicity of lifestyle, compassion for poor people and passion for justice must speak loudly about the higher call we are following.
>
> Thank you for walking in Christ's shoes and serving him by serving the least this year.

Chapter 7

Speaking Out

The Evangelical Alliance Relief Fund was created to extend compassionate aid to people in distress: a simple response to often complex problems. Surprisingly, however, even its first leaflet, published in 1967, recognised that this was not the whole solution to the world's needs. In the wake of the Bihar famine in India it said:

> Monsoon failure in both 1965 and 1966 caused famine in several States, with a population totalling 60 millions. Millions of lives could be lost. Ultimately the matter can only be resolved at the national and

In 2006 Tearfund was part of the Stop Climate Chaos coalition's campaign on climate change issues. Eight-year-old Tearfund supporter Daniel Causebrook was one of six young people who delivered more than 150,000 pledge cards to the Prime Minister.

international level; there is a call here for Christians to play their full part in influencing national policies both from inside and outside political life.

The surprise here is that it challenges Christians to influence national policies for the benefit of the poor – a degree of political engagement that was not characteristic of evangelicals at the time.

It was reading a Sunday newspaper article about the famine in Bihar that first caught at Mary Jean Duffield's heart and made her want to do something about inequality and suffering. When she joined the first Tearfund committee in 1968, she found herself out of step with her colleagues over a national campaign to press the government to fulfil its commitment to increase overseas aid. Four decades later she recalled:

Burkina Faso, 2005: Growing cotton can provide a living for many people in poor countries, but international trade rules can harm their livelihoods. For Tearfund, it is important not just to treat the symptoms of poverty but to address the underlying issues.

Traffic lights

It seems clear ... that genuine Christian social concern will embrace both social service and social action. It would be very artificial to divorce them. Some cases of need cannot be relieved at all without political action (the harsh treatment of slaves could be ameliorated, but not slavery itself; it had to be abolished). To go on relieving other needs, though necessary, may condone the situation which causes them. If travellers on the Jerusalem-Jericho road were habitually beaten up, and habitually cared for by Good Samaritans, the need for better laws to eliminate armed robbery might well be overlooked. If road accidents keep happening at a particular crossroads, it is not more ambulances that are needed but the installation of traffic lights to prevent accidents. It is always good to feed the hungry; it is better if possible to eradicate the causes of hunger. So if we truly love our neighbours, and want to serve them, our service may oblige us to take (or solicit) political action on their behalf.

John Stott, *Issues facing Christians today*, 1984

I thought that we should back the campaign, and I thought we should get our constituency to campaign for it. I also wanted us to have an ethical investment fund. I felt we had to try to change the sources of poverty.

More experienced heads on the committee were concerned, however, about how the evangelical constituency would view it if Tearfund took a 'political' stance – to Mary Jean's obvious disappointment:

I was by far the youngest – I was LSE, class of '68, when it was at its most radical, and I think there was bound to be a sort of clash. I think it was quite a conservative committee and perhaps they were right, perhaps the important thing was to grow the Fund. I think there was a whole group in the evangelical world that was frightened of the label 'left wing' – right from the top it seemed there was a fear of going back to basics, of asking difficult questions. There was a sense that this is something very complicated, we just don't want to get involved with it.

Although she would later resign from the committee early in its life, in July 1970, Mary Jean's presence in this formative phase undoubtedly had a catalytic effect, prompting discussion of issues which might otherwise have been left to one side. As Morgan Derham later recognised, 'She did us a lot of good, because most of us were rather starchy right-wingers.'

In 1997 Tearfund highlighted the destructive impact of international debt on Zambia, where nine out of ten farmers were living in absolute poverty. Their average cash income had fallen from £150 in 1985 to just £17. By 2005, years of international campaigning had won substantial cuts in Zambia's debt, freeing up money for improved education and healthcare.

In January 1969 the committee considered her paper on political involvement, which recommended setting up a group to study the role of Christians with regard to policies critically influencing world poverty. It also suggested identifying ways for Christians to make their support of these policies effective.

It was not yet time, however, for Tearfund to engage wholeheartedly in campaigning, and while the committee agreed that 'Christians may have to take a lead to persuade the government to send more aid', it questioned whether 'agitation' was 'the right emphasis for the Christian church'. Nevertheless, it was agreed that Tearfund should publicise the facts and figures and underline the needs.

Later that year, the committee faced a dilemma: should Tearfund align itself with the 'National Sign-In on World Poverty'? This interdenominational campaign was calling on the government to fulfil its 1968 pledge to raise British public and private funds for developing countries to 1 per cent of Gross National Product by 1972 (of which 0.7 per cent was to be official aid).

Christians in action: Honduras

A 1991 logging agreement with a US corporation by the government of Honduras signed away more than 1 million hectares of virgin forest and put the indigenous Miskito Indian population's way of life in jeopardy. Tearfund's partner Mopawi took up their case with government officials, and Tearfund brought an international dimension to the campaign by writing to the Honduran government and asking supporters to do the same in defence of the Indians' rights.

The following year, the Miskito Indians were able to celebrate a victory: the campaign had succeeded, with the Honduran government overturning the agreement.

In 1998 the people faced another challenge. Plans were revealed for the construction of a hydro-electric dam on the Patuca River in the heart of this region, threatening further destruction. The dam would prevent the river flooding, thus preventing fertilisation of the land and reducing food production, while a new road would open up the region to inward migration, putting the local people's land rights under threat. Once again Mopawi launched a campaign. The community, with its previous experience of standing up against the powerful, was now quick to mobilise. Tearfund joined in, asking its supporters to write to the President of Honduras in support of the indigenous people's rights.

In March 1999 the companies involved withdrew from the dam project, citing the level of local opposition.

The committee was divided over whether to mobilise Tearfund's supporters, and those members who worried that the campaign was too 'political' and might have too 'left-wing' an emphasis for most of Tearfund's constituency prevailed. Tearfund did not join the campaign, but it did express its support for the cause.

> **S**peak up for those who cannot speak for themselves, for the rights of all who are destitute. Speak up and judge fairly; defend the rights of the poor and needy. (Proverbs 31:8–9)

The overseas aid target in question was as challenging then as for many years following. In 1969 Britain's foreign aid amounted to £150m, just 0.42 per cent of Gross National Product. About 90 per cent of this aid took the form of grants and loans to governments of developing countries, and almost 58 per cent of it had to be spent on buying goods and services from the UK.

Even in those days, debt was an issue: two-thirds of all aid in any one year was needed to pay back outstanding loans and interest on previous aid programmes. Tearfund warned that by 1980, unless aid increased significantly, the total aid programme would be offset by such repayments. It called on its supporters to pray for the UK government and for Third World leaders.

Tearfund's December 1969 insert in the *Church of England Newspaper* asked supporters to raise these global issues with those in power, particularly by writing letters:

> At the appropriate time and through the appropriate channel, Christians have a responsibility to exercise their democratic right as members of society to express their convictions and their concern.
>
> First there's your Member of Parliament. MPs do take notice of letters that express concern regarding social issues, international relationships and the country's finances ... and the subject of international aid involves all three.
>
> Then there is the newspaper world – both the national dailies and your local weekly. And along with these your church or organisation's magazine, together with other publications and periodicals.

So while it may have recoiled from Mary Jean's radicalism and felt the shadow of evangelical conservatism at its shoulder, Tearfund did from the outset encourage its supporters to do their best to influence government policy on global poverty. Stephen Rand recalls that this was a significant part of Tearfund's early stance:

Tearfund went through a period of being thought to be incredibly conservative, but for example there was an early filmstrip, *How poor is the rich man*, which included a whole chunk about the vital importance of influencing Parliament and writing to your MP. In fact the script could be put out today and would not look dated.

During the 1970s Tearfund continued to speak out from time to time, drawing attention to the wider issues of injustice that lay behind poverty – such as unfair trading systems which condemned people to poverty. No relief or development programme could undo the harm that such policies did to millions of people.

Each time it considered speaking out on what were deemed 'political' issues, however, there was still a tightrope to walk. On the one hand there was concern about whether too much activity of this kind would draw unfavourable attention from the Charity Commission. In the 1970s the Commission was still taking the view that to seek to influence voters on political matters or to campaign for a change in the law fell outside the remit of a charity, and charities regularly had their knuckles rapped for straying from legitimate 'education' into illegitimate 'propaganda'. On the other hand, there was the delicate balance between educating the supporters and yet not alienating them: how willing was the evangelical constituency to embark on such a course of action?

Influence

As Christians we are supposed to be the salt of our society, and we in Britain live in a free society where we can influence public opinion and government policy. We have a responsibility to act if we see our government or banks or companies going against what we read in God's word. This may involve us in lobbying our Members of Parliament or in some other way taking positive action. We may feel insignificant and that we can do very little but imagine the feeling of the boy who offered his loaves and fishes to Jesus, and then saw them used to feed a huge crowd of people.

Each one of us has a responsibility to offer up our lives and all we have to the Lord and to let him teach us from his word how we should live. And we need to remember the importance that God places on caring for the oppressed. 'If you put an end to oppression, to every gesture of contempt, and to every evil word; if you give food to the hungry and satisfy those who are in need, then the darkness around you will turn to the brightness of noon. And I will always guide you and satisfy you with good things.'

From *How poor is the rich man*, 1970s Tearfund filmstrip

Tanzania, 2005: Esther Ng'enula harvests her family's food supply. In that year, Tearfund was part of the Make Poverty History campaign, calling for debt cancellation and more and better aid for countries like Tanzania.

Tearfund knew its vision was appealing to a developing radical consciousness among evangelical Christians, but it also sensed that the greater part of its constituency probably shared its own wariness of a Christian organisation becoming embroiled in 'politics'.

Part of the solution lay in another organisation: the World Development Movement (WDM), a campaigning group formed in 1970. In 1973, for example, when WDM was running a campaign on government overseas aid and defence expenditure, Tearfund felt it lacked the necessary information to take action of its own, but should direct supporters' enquiries to WDM. This option offered Tearfund a way to mobilise its supporters on political issues without having to take a more overtly political stance. It was thus a way of avoiding potential criticism from supporters, but was recognition that Tearfund had neither the expertise nor the resources to research and substantiate its own campaigns.

The 1980s opened with a landmark international document, the Brandt Report, *North South: a programme for survival*. Published in March 1980, it was a challenging appeal to end world poverty, calling for 'a commitment to international social justice'. It focused on the need for more and better aid, action on Third World debt, and removal of rich countries' tariffs and other barriers to Third World manufactured goods.

When the report was discussed by a summit of world leaders in Mexico in October 1981, Tearfund's response was quite outspoken. Writing in *Third Way* magazine in February 1982, George Hoffman described the meeting as a 'pantomime' characterised by the 'posturing performances' of world leaders, and criticised the conference for failing to tackle the issues in a more realistic and responsible manner.

He called for governments to meet the Brandt Report's demands and cited Psalm 146:7: God was not only the one who provided food

London, October 1985: Tearfund supporters join the World Development Movement's mass lobby of Parliament calling for action on world poverty and hunger.

Prophetic well-drilling

“ When we go to a village to drill for water, we do two surveys. We do a socio-economic survey to find out where the poorest and most marginalised people live – these are the outcasts, or *dalits*. Then we do the physical survey, to find out where the water is located. If the result shows a water source where the *dalits* live, we drill the well there. That means that the higher-caste women will have to come to this community to get their water. If we drilled it in the high-caste area, they would fence it off and not allow the poor people to touch it.

It's a powerful tool. At first these women are quite upset that the water point has been drilled among the poor people who they still think are untouchable. But then they begin to see that they have to forget those old prejudices. ”

Dino Touthang, Executive Director, EFICOR, India

for the hungry; he was also the defender of the poor, the one who 'executes judgment for the oppressed'. He concluded: 'And for many, their hunger will never be satisfied until justice for the oppressed has been executed in their land.'

Three years later, in October 1985, 20,000 people attended a mass lobby of Parliament coordinated by WDM and supported by churches and development agencies, including Tearfund. The event coincided with the first anniversary of BBC Television's historic reports of famine in Ethiopia. Its aim was to urge government action to prevent future famine, and WDM estimated that 90 per cent of

Christians in action: Peru

In 1985, at the height of Peru's civil war between the government and Shining Path guerrillas, lawyer Alfonso Wieland, who would later become executive chairman of Tearfund's partner, Peace and Hope, paid his first visit to a prison. Here he found prisoners, including pastors, held on false charges of collaboration with the guerrillas, ordinary people caught up in a fierce conflict and suffering injustice at the hands of the powerful and the violent. He wrote in his book *In love with his justice*:

> That Sunday was a turning point for me. My life would never be the same, nor my faith. My understanding of God had changed. I had been converted to his justice.

Today, Peace and Hope works to defend people whose social status denies them justice. It believes that because all people are created in the image of God, everyone is of equal worth. Alfonso Wieland notes:

> The work of Peace and Hope is based on the biblical concept of justice. We understand this to mean making human rights possible for all, as well as restoring good relationships between God, his people and creation. We believe that biblical justice demands the defence of the poor, as they are at a disadvantage and often defenceless in society. Working for justice means building a society which affirms the rights and responsibilities of all people.
>
> Peace and Hope works to help change institutions and legal systems that go against human rights. In this way it hopes to improve the administration of justice in Peru.

Peace and Hope offers free legal help to people or communities that are victims of human rights abuse, and provides legal, psychological and pastoral support for victims of violence, particularly women and children. It also helps to educate communities about their rights, so that they can take action to challenge unjust systems and practices in the state.

Faces

❝ In the end, injustice has real faces, victims who suffer in their own flesh the mistaken policies of the authorities. And it is from these real cases that we can teach the church about the importance of working for social justice… It is the task of the body of Christ as a whole. ❞

Alfonso Wieland, *In love with his justice*, 2003

MPs from English constituencies were lobbied. The day before the lobby, *The Times* had published a letter from leaders of aid agencies, including Tearfund, pressing the government to make every effort to tackle world poverty and hunger, the scale of which was 'beyond the scope of voluntary agencies'. The letter concluded:

We therefore urge MPs of all parties to press for immediate government action to increase aid to the poorest people; to give much more support to local food production which benefits the poor; to provide fairer trading opportunities especially for the poorest countries; and to reduce the debt burden which weighs so heavily on the poor.

According to a report in *Tear Times*, George Hoffman, who represented Tearfund at the mass meeting accompanying the lobby, gave full backing to the call:

Christians should stand up and speak out on behalf of the poor and oppressed who have no voice. As Christians we enjoy the freedom of a democratic society – and that means we have certain responsibilities. Part of that responsibility is to watch the way in which Government funds are allocated on our behalf.

Tear Fund thus fully endorses the representation that is being made on an all-party platform in full co-operation with other agencies to ensure that the maximum contributions are made to meet the needs of the poorer countries of the world.

Signs

❝ Localised actions are signs of the kingdom. They give me hope because they point towards a future of justice and peace. The kingdom has already come, not in its fullness, that is quite clear, but God is in action and we are called to be signs of the kingdom, doers of justice. ❞

René Padilla, Tearfund's International President 1998–2007

Although it's a cliché, it's still true: 'Evil triumphs when good men do nothing.' Obscenities such as poverty and starvation will continue unless we speak out and speak up. This year we have celebrated the centenary of Lord Shaftesbury's death. As an evangelical politician he achieved more than any other man for the reformation of our society. As Christians we must uphold that inheritance.

Later that year, Tearfund's Christmas appeal for Africa didn't focus only on the familiar themes of drought, famine, sickness and death. This Christmas, it said, 'Tear Fund is emphasising that we in the developed countries of the North benefit from an unjust system of international trade and finance':

> Third World countries are thwarted in their fight against poverty by a world economic system set against them. Today's unjust international trade practices are the results of the rich North pursuing policies of national self-interest over the years. The injustice of the system can be seen in the food mountains of the European Community, in the trade patterns heavily biased in favour of the North, in the dubious practices of some multinational companies, and in the sometimes self-interested conditions of Government aid. But from a biblical viewpoint, structural injustice is a symptom of sin in a fallen world.

Tearfund was an Internet pioneer among Christian organisations – and its first web presence was a campaign. In 1995 it provided a couple of pages of text and images for the newly launched Church Net UK website. The material featured Tearfund's campaign to protect the Honduras rainforest. The following year Tearfund launched its own website.

Tearfund was becoming more vocal on the need to address the structural issues underlying poverty. In 1992, Tearfund and British Youth for Christ joined with Spring Harvest to launch the Whose Earth? campaign to educate Christians about environmental damage and to raise funds for environmental projects overseas. There was still scepticism to overcome, particularly among evangelical Christians, and Tearfund had to tread carefully, distancing itself from what were perceived as 'New Age' notions about care for the environment and emphasising the biblical duty of stewardship.

The campaign was linked to the UN's Earth Summit, an international conference on the environment held that year in Rio de Janeiro, Brazil, and it culminated in a mass picnic in Hyde Park, London, in September.

London, 1992: Delivering Tearfund's Whose Earth? campaign petition to the Prime Minister.

In other parts of the world, meanwhile, evangelical Christian groups with which Tearfund worked in partnership were reaching

their own conclusions about the appropriateness of campaigning action – and often in the face of more imminent threats.

In Honduras, for example, Mopawi had been working for several years with the people of the Mosquitia region in development, but also helping to protect their rights against powerful government and commercial interests that threatened their way of life. When the government signed a logging deal with a US multinational in 1991, Mopawi launched a major campaign to get it overturned.

In Peru, the 1980s and 1990s brought a bloody civil war between the government and Shining Path guerrillas, in which up to 69,000 people were killed. Many people 'disappeared' or were falsely imprisoned. In the face of widespread injustice and abuses, a small group of evangelical Christians set up Peace and Hope, an organisation working to secure justice for poor and vulnerable people who would otherwise be denied it. Alfonso Wieland was a lawyer who got involved and later became Director of Peace and Hope:

Peru, 1998: The freak weather caused by El Niño brought flooding to families in the shanty towns of Lima, Peru. Tearfund partners gave practical help to the poor, and at the same time worked to tackle wider issues of injustice and human rights abuse.

I was involved in this moment of Peru's history, so as a Christian I asked God what I should do. I understood that God has a passion for justice, and I was convinced that there is a special call from God not just for lawyers but for all Christians and the church to bring justice to the oppressed and the needy.

The experience of its partners here and in other parts of the world presented a number of challenges to Tearfund. They were engaged in bold and resolute action, taking on government and big business in obedience to the biblical injunction to defend the rights of the poor and needy. Their success was based not only on vision and commitment, but also on expertise, reliable and accurate research, and a willingness to hold governments and other centres of power to account. If Tearfund was to help them, it would need to equip itself properly, and in the 1990s there was a growing momentum within the organisation to get to the point where it could mount effective campaigning which was well-grounded in reliable information, biblically-based and successfully communicated – and which had a distinctively Christian nature. Stephen Rand recalled:

> **D**efend the cause of the weak and fatherless; maintain the rights of the poor and oppressed. Rescue the weak and needy; deliver them from the hand of the wicked. (Psalm 82:3–4)

I thought it was vital that Tearfund should begin to do campaigning. To me, there was a fatal flaw in the argument for sending people to WDM, because WDM did their campaigning on an entirely secular basis despite the fact that most of their supporters were Christians. That meant there was nobody engaging with the question of how we could pray about these issues, and I believed that change comes about not simply by getting governments to do the right thing: there is a spiritual battle involved too.

Justice

Justice is not just a human interest of a few; it is one of the traits of God's character. God is a God of justice. He loves justice. God demands justice. He expects justice. In Jesus Christ he has entered into human history to make justice possible and I think that one aspect of being a Christian means to be involved in working towards a world that reflects God's justice as well as God's love.
René Padilla, Tearfund's International President 1998-2007

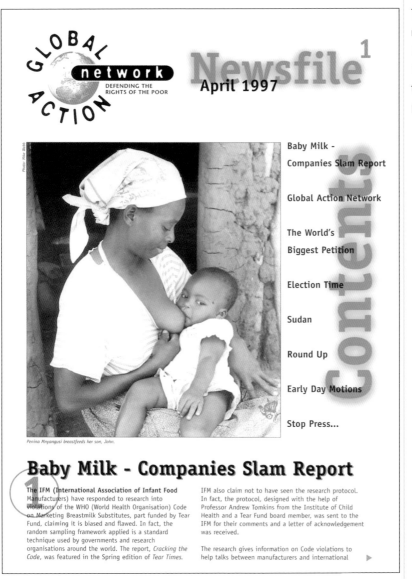

Penina Mnyangusi breastfeeds her son, John.

Baby Milk - Companies Slam Report

The IFM (International Association of Infant Food Manufacturers) have responded to research into violations of the WHO (World Health Organisation) Code on Marketing Breastmilk Substitutes, part funded by Tear Fund, claiming it is biased and flawed. In fact, the random sampling framework applied is a standard technique used by governments and research organisations around the world. The report, *Cracking the Code*, was featured in the Spring edition of *Tear Times*.

IFM also claim not to have seen the research protocol. In fact, the protocol, designed with the help of Professor Andrew Tomkins from the Institute of Child Health and a Tear Fund board member, was sent to the IFM for their comments and a letter of acknowledgement was received.

The research gives information on Code violations to help talks between manufacturers and international ▶

Tearfund's campaigning magazine *Global Action Network* was launched in 1997. Its first issue targeted the issue of powdered milk for babies.

The first step was to appoint someone to the staff who would specialise in researching some of the key campaigning issues, so that Tearfund could at least explain them competently to its supporters. Theologian Tim Chester, later to become Tearfund's Policy Director, joined in 1993 with a brief to tackle these issues in *Tear Times*. Stephen Rand recalled:

The Jubilee 2000 campaign called for the cancellation of poor countries' unpayable debt. Tearfund mobilised its supporters to get behind the campaign, motivated by a biblical vision of justice for the poor.

For Tearfund to get into this we needed to bring our supporters with us, and so we needed to start educating them about the structural issues, and why it was important to do something. Tim's articles were about showing people the bigger context within which Tearfund's work was set, and this prepared the ground for starting our own campaigning.

Jubilee 2000

It was breathtaking. Literally. It stopped the world in its tracks. When churches started demonstrating on debt, governments listened – and acted. When churches starting organising, petitioning, and even – that most unholy of acts today, God forbid, lobbying ... on AIDS and global health, governments listened – and acted. I'm here today in all humility to say: you changed minds; you changed policy; you changed the world.

U2 singer **Bono** addressing the **National Prayer Breakfast, Washington DC, 2 February 2006**, on Jubilee 2000

World Watch Prayer Link was launched at the end of 1992, a monthly prayer update enabling supporters to pray in an informed way for topics of international concern. In 1997, *Global Action Network* became Tearfund's first full-scale programme of equipping supporters to campaign on poverty issues from a biblical basis. Its first action was to urge supporters to get behind the Jubilee 2000 campaign to cancel unpayable international debt.

Jubilee 2000 marked a watershed in Tearfund's growing engagement with advocacy. The campaign had a Tearfund link in its origins: one of the key people involved in its start was Isabel Carter, editor of Tearfund's *Footsteps* magazine. Flying across Africa in 1994, she felt God gave her a vision that by the year 2000 the injustice of crippling international debt should be resolved. On her return, she linked up with veteran debt campaigners Bill Peters and Martin Dent, who had

Causes

Tearfund supporters – show the generosity, the compassion, the care, but sometimes you can't just keep pulling bodies out of the river; you've got to send somebody upstream to see what or who is throwing them in.

Jim Wallis, *Tear Times*, 2006

been advocating the same idea since 1990, and then Ann Pettifor of the Debt Crisis Network. With help from some individual Tearfund staff and others, the push began to make Jubilee 2000 a reality, and in 1996 Isabel secured charitable status and some initial funding.

The earth is the Lord's, and everything in it, the world, and all who live in it. (Psalm 24:1)

At first, like a number of other agencies, Tearfund was hesitant to take on such a huge venture by itself: it would not have had the capacity to make it happen. Not for the first time, moreover, there was controversy and debate within the organisation – but this time it proved a catalyst for radical commitment. David Westlake joined Tearfund as Youth Director in 1996:

In 1999 Tearfund broke new ground by arranging a live webcast via the Internet linking Chancellor of the Exchequer Gordon Brown in London with Elinata Kasanga, a poor farmer in Zambia, as part of the Jubilee 2000 campaign. Their conversation, covered by the BBC, ITN and Reuters, meant Elinata had the opportunity to explain directly to the Chancellor the impact unpayable debt was having on her life. *Tear Times* editor Mike Webb recalled: 'It was a lot of hard work but we managed to do it with God's grace and help. To me it really symbolised something about Tearfund: it was giving a voice to the voiceless.' In 2005 Tearfund repeated the event, this time as part of the Make Poverty History campaign in the run-up to the G8 meeting.

Very soon after I joined Tearfund, there was the big discussion as to whether it should get involved in the Jubilee 2000 campaign. I remember great angst about whether this was too political: would our supporters accept it? There was a great wrestling with these issues, and I think we realised our supporters were more educated than we maybe gave them credit for – people now understood that decisions by governments and agencies like the IMF and the World Bank had a massive impact on the lives of poor communities, and that to influence them was just as important as doing an immunisation programme.

Prayer

Prayer is powerful; prayer is political; prayer changes things.
Jim Wallis

I think we also grew in confidence about saying what we believed: that serving the poor and seeking God's heart for justice isn't an optional add-on, it's an essential part of being a Christian. We began to take more risks across the whole of Tearfund.

Isabel Carter also saw it as a turning point for Tearfund:

Jubilee 2000 in the early years was an amazing story of God at work. It was such a privilege, stepping out in faith, all the time having to take risks and trust God. Individuals in Tearfund were fantastically supportive, and over time Tearfund's position changed quite substantially. When Jubilee 2000 was formed as a charity, Tearfund was great because it sent out a flyer in *Tear Times*, which was a huge, huge boost, and that was a really concrete sign of solidarity within Tearfund.

Then two years on, when the Jubilee 2000 coalition was set up, Tearfund came very firmly on board, becoming a founder member of the coalition, and was very enthusiastically taking the whole idea forward. But I think the debate within Tearfund about whether it should support Jubilee 2000 was the beginning of a big change. It really challenged Tearfund to think again about its position on campaigning. Now Tearfund's advocacy work is fantastic, and having a real impact in the world.

An early contribution by Tearfund was to ask its supporters to gather signatures for the Jubilee 2000 petition outside polling booths during the 10 June 1999 European elections. The Sign of Hope campaign resulted in a record-breaking 232,927 signatures collected in one day, which created a lasting reputation for Tearfund in the world of campaigning as an agency that could deliver what it promised.

Stephen Rand, Tearfund's Communications Director at the time, was deeply involved in its relationship with Jubilee 2000, and saw the campaign's emergence, growth and success as a significant move of God. He later recalled:

Tearfund supporters joined the Make Poverty History march in Edinburgh in 2005 to call on leaders of the world's most powerful countries for more and better aid, debt relief and trade justice. In the run-up to the event, 97,000 Tearfund supporters sent postcards to the Prime Minister asking for decisive action.

The coming together of Isabel, Bill, Martin and Ann was really a 'God moment'. And in terms of how God moves, Jubilee 2000 is fascinating because it is a point at which the church becomes completely integrated in a wider movement for change. It was never particularly seen as a 'church' thing, but everyone knows the church was at the heart of it.

I think Tearfund's emergence into the whole world of public policy

and campaigning was entirely built around our involvement with Jubilee 2000.

Jubilee 2000 marked another stage in Tearfund's process of coming 'out of the ghetto'. It had demonstrated that it could participate in a broad coalition for justice without needing to conceal or compromise its Christian ethos and motivation. As it had found in its disaster response and development work, so too in its campaigning it found that its Christian distinctives were actually its greatest strength. This created a foundation for a significant expansion of Tearfund's campaigning and advocacy work.

Praying and campaigning

    Praying is not the least we can do: it is the most. God invented justice and cares about poor people infinitely more than we do, so we know we're talking to the one who has the power to act. In campaigning, we call on our leaders to bring about justice, but we also pray for them. We pray for church leaders and people who work with Tearfund from churches overseas when they meet with governments to champion poor communities.

How to be part of a miracle, Tearfund, 2007

At the start of the twenty-first century, unclean water was the world's second biggest killer of children, with some 1.8 million children dying every year from water-borne diseases. For more than a billion people in the world, access to clean water remained a dream. Tearfund has enabled poor communities to achieve clean water supplies since its earliest days, and its campaigning and advocacy work has secured change at the international policy level that benefits poor people worldwide.

Meanwhile, in 1997 the organisation had appointed its first full-time public policy adviser – Andy Atkins, who became Advocacy Director in 2000. On joining Tearfund, he was charged with drawing up a plan to make advocacy a long-term mainstream strategy for the organisation. Over the next few years Tearfund developed for the first time a team of policy specialists and campaigners. As the new

Tearfund campaigners turned out in force at the I Count rally in Trafalgar Square in November 2006, among 25,000 people calling for urgent action on climate change. Tearfund's UK President Elaine Storkey said, 'The Bible says that you should love the Lord your God with all your heart, mind, soul and strength, and your neighbour as yourself, and if you believe that, then you just have to be here today.'

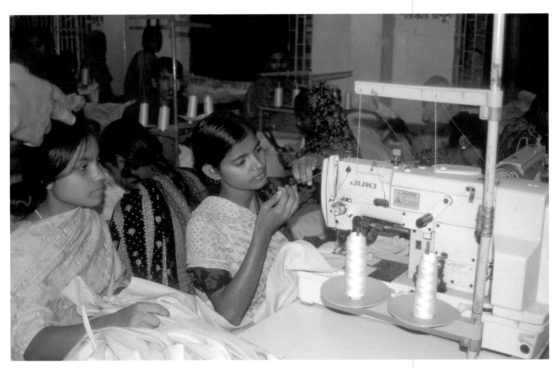

century began, this enabled it to play a key role in Make Poverty History and a range of campaigns on issues including global poverty, trade justice and climate change, as well as supporting overseas partners in their national and regional advocacy initiatives. It became more common to hear and see Tearfund in the news media as an expert and credible voice in its field.

Tearfund also began to achieve recognised success in advocacy at an international level, as Andy Atkins recalled:

> The World Summit on Sustainable Development in 2002 agreed a new international target for providing sanitation for poor people, widely seen as the major outcome of the summit. It happened as a result of Tearfund working very closely with the government's Department for International Development. They in turn persuaded the EU to make it one of their main objectives, and the EU then negotiated with everyone else and refused to back down until the Americans finally agreed.
>
> In 2005 Secretary of State Hilary Benn announced a doubling of UK aid for water, and he specifically referred to lobbying by Tearfund and Water Aid as having convinced the government of the need to do that. What's also interesting is that in 2006 they doubled it again – £200 million a year of UK aid going just to water. Tearfund's entire annual

Tearfund's Lift the Label campaign, launched in 2003, drew attention to the conditions in which garment workers in poor countries have to work. The campaign challenged supporters to think about how our consumer choices in fashion, food and finance impact the lives of some of the poorest people in the world.

budget in that year was around £50 million. So by lobbying the UK government we'd seen them increase the money they were going to give to water to four times Tearfund's entire budget. That is the kind of result you can get from well-directed advocacy.

Advocacy has become one of the key elements in Tearfund's work – a recognition that while helping people to overcome the effects of poverty at the local level, it also needs to engage with the global structural issues that undergird poverty. The foundation of all this work is the biblical mandate of Proverbs 31:8–9: 'Speak up for those who cannot speak for themselves, for the rights of all who are destitute. Speak up and judge fairly; defend the rights of the poor and needy.' And as Andy Atkins notes, the more sophisticated Tearfund's advocacy work becomes, the more it needs to be grounded in prayer:

> **S**eek justice, encourage the oppressed. Defend the cause of the fatherless, plead the case of the widow.
> (Isaiah 1:17)

When we were campaigning as part of the Trade Justice Movement in 2005 we set up a 24/7 prayer network with our overseas partners. To me that was a lovely picture of how prayer should be: Christians around the world connected up, praying for the same thing in their own way, in their own place, but all of it coming together before God. We will never know the power of this, but we believe and we see the evidence of its impact.

When we go into tough meetings with political leaders, it's just wonderful to know people are praying for us. We can use all our knowledge and education to decide what we think is right, but at the end of the day we have to listen to God and to what he thinks. I've learnt that on my own I'm not going to change the UN or the World Bank – we need perseverance and enormous Christian hope, and a belief that the result is in God's hands.

We do our bit and we pray for guidance in doing that. We pray even more for God to do the rest.

Chapter 8

A Vision and a Mission

For forty years Tearfund has been motivated by a vision. At its simplest, it has been a vision to see the Kingdom of God come, to see people experiencing the 'fullness of life' which Jesus promised (John 10:10) and the church worldwide being good news to the poor in word and deed. What made Tearfund stand out and command attention in the Christian world originally was its emphasis on the practical alleviation of poverty and suffering in the name of Christ: the church being his hands as well as his voice. The commitment of Tearfund and its partners worldwide to serve poor communities in this way was summed up by the simple slogan 'God's love in action'.

Those forty years have also seen a growth in Tearfund's understanding of its mission – which in turn has had a widespread and positive influence on thinking and ministry in the church.

In the early days, while Tearfund fought and increasingly won the argument about the legitimacy of social action as an expression of Christian discipleship, 'social action' and 'evangelism' still tended to be seen as complementary, rather than integrated, activities. The metaphor of scissors was commonly used, for example by David Watson in 1982:

Wholehearted

I guess with Tearfund we want it all. We want to be wholeheartedly loving Jesus and full of the Spirit and passionate about the Bible and worship and church and discipleship and evangelism, and we also are passionate about caring for the poor and the outcast, the widow and the orphan. It has to come together. If we can get that together it will be the salvation of the church in the west as well as for poor communities around the world.
David Westlake, Tearfund 1996–

I have come to see that the spiritual gospel and the social gospel, to use those words for the moment, are like the two blades of a pair of scissors. If you lose either, you have lost your cutting edge! To keep the cutting edge of the gospel, you need both.

Tearfund's work in development and emergency relief is aimed at helping people overcome the effects of poverty and disaster – and experience economic, social, emotional and spiritual transformation in their lives.

For some, however, the implicit assumption was that for Christians to help a poor community to improve its water supply, healthcare or living conditions was only truly justified if it resulted in conversions. Tearfund tried to push people beyond this.

Writing in *Tear Times* in 1976, Deputy Director Bill Latham said Tearfund was 'frequently asked whether there is spiritual fruit from its projects. The question implies a "means-to-an-evangelistic-end" motivation rather than compassionate service which in itself is part and parcel of our Christian responsibility.' 'But,' he continued, 'sometimes the Lord does use relief and development programmes that are carried out in His name to break down barriers. Love in action is often irresistible.'

He cited a water project he had visited in Guinea Bissau, where as a result of a well being sunk with the help of a Tearfund grant, two village chiefs burned their idols and committed their lives to Christ. In the same issue, consultant Alan Norrish, reporting on well-drilling pro-grammes in Ethiopia, said that what distin-guished Christian aid workers was that they

Integral mission

To talk about integral mission is to talk about God's purpose to reshape the whole of human life wherever Christians are.
René Padilla, Tearfund's International President 1998–2007

Inseparable

‟ Actions that show God's concern for love and justice are inseparable from the proclamation of the gospel. ”

René Padilla, Tearfund's International President 1998–2007

had hope and the power of God at work in them: 'The love of Christ constrains us and that makes all the difference.'

The experience of local Christian partners working with poor communities around the world steadily influenced and shaped Tearfund's understanding. For many of them, faced with the reality of poverty and injustice on their doorstep, the relationship between 'evangelism' and 'social action' was not an abstract theoretical debate but an everyday experience. These activities were indivisible aspects of the church's mission to bring the gospel of Jesus to the world.

In 1975, *Tear Times* quoted Saúl Gómez Díaz, President of

The predominantly Buddhist country of Cambodia is still scarred by the terror and mass killings of the communist Khmer Rouge regime in the 1970s. Now, as Tearfund's Christian partner groups express the love of Christ in practical ways among poor and marginalised people, new cell churches are springing up.

Do something

❝ James tells us that our faith should be seen through our good works, and I believe that also means that if you see a person who is suffering, who is hungry, you don't just say, 'Oh, let's pray.' You actually do something about it. That to me is integral mission. ❞
Anthony Poggo, Executive Director, Across, Sudan

Tearfund partner CEDEN in Honduras, where Hurricane Fifi had left 600,000 people homeless:

> Jesus saw and ministered to man as a whole. He saw to the needs of the soul and spirit as well as of the body. He came so that man could have life in all its fullness.

In Costa Rica, Jonas Gonzales was leader of Goodwill Caravans, a combined ministry of development, literacy and evangelism that was engaged in relief and rehabilitation work after floods had ravaged low-lying areas:

Prayer

❝ I've been on the staff since 1987, and I would say that Tearfund is more prayerful now than it has ever been. ❞
Dewi Hughes, Tearfund 1987–

> We believe that the human being is a unity with multiple manifestations and we believe that only the integral ministry for the total man fulfils the will of our Lord Jesus Christ in relation to man's needs.

Tearfund, however, still had some way to travel towards a vision of truly 'integral ministry'. In UK circles, having established the principle that the church should be engaged in practical measures to relieve poverty and suffering through relief and development, Tearfund now faced the perception that it was not supporting the whole ministry of the church. As Graham Fairbairn later recalled:

Seek justice, encourage the oppressed. (Isaiah 1:17)

> It was felt that we needed to engage with all the things the church needed: leadership training, support in evangelism and so on. There wasn't a lot of philosophical debate around Tearfund in those days, but there was a clear view that we needed to support the church.

The result was the creation of a new department in 1979: Evangelism and Christian Education, headed by Ernest Oliver. Its purpose was to fund projects related to evangelistic activities, church planting and growth, media ministries, literature, theological education and pastoral training – everything from enabling an African pastor to complete a theology degree in London to providing an Egyptian evangelist with a motorcycle so he could visit villages and tell people about Jesus. In a way, of course, the creation of a separate department within Tearfund to fund 'evangelistic activities' replicated the old conceptual dichotomy, and in 1992 it was reintegrated with the other aspects of Tearfund's development work.

The debate continued, however: should 'evangelism' and 'social

Church

❝ The need is so great, but the answer has been given to us: it's the local church. The thing about the church is it doesn't go away. Because we are the church, we are always close to the community, enabling people to step out of poverty and bringing them to faith. I see its effects day by day. ❞
Cuthbert Gondwe, Eagles, Malawi

For the nomadic Tuareg people of North Africa, climate change is making life harder. Tearfund's partner Jemed has worked with them, distributing emergency food when rains failed, and helping them to dig wells and protect pastureland from the encroaching desert. Jemed's service has built trust, and a number of people have come to faith in Christ.

In 2001 the UN reported that HIV was spreading faster in the former Soviet Union than anywhere else in the world. By 2006, more than 1.5 million people had HIV in Russia. Tearfund's Christian partners were visiting schools, prisons and drug rehab centres to teach people about HIV and demonstrating the benefits of an alternative lifestyle – Jesus' promise of life in all its fullness.

action' be seen as complementary or integrated, whether within an organisation such as Tearfund or on a local, national or international church level? As Stephen Rand put it,

> There were varying degrees of integration and separation. In some cases, Tearfund was working with Christian NGOs that were specifically social action organisations, so they were doing the relief work while another part of their denomination was doing the evangelism. I think there were some people who would even have argued that if

Transformation

❝ I like Tearfund's strategy of very centrally focusing on the local church. That is really powerful, because the local church is an agent for transformation in a community. And if we empower the local church we'll be able to go a long way in addressing the social needs of the people. We want to work with Tearfund; we appreciate it. ❞

Francis Mkandawire, General Secretary, Evangelical Association of Malawi

Good news

❝ Jesus came and fed the hungry and healed the sick. Good news is not just preaching: it's practising. Telling the story of God's love, of creation and salvation, is wonderful but if it is not linked to actions it is not complete. The good news has to be integral. ❞

Osvaldo Munguia, Director, Mopawi, Honduras

Tearfund was supporting a development project in a country and there were Christians doing 'spiritual' work elsewhere in the same country, that was still integral because the 'two blades of the scissors' were seen on a national basis rather than on an individual project basis.

What seemed to be missing was the idea that Christians would do relief and development work in a distinctively different way than non-Christians because of the mission of the church.

For Stephen, who spent several years communicating Tearfund's work and vision, the key issue was not about a theoretical divide between 'evangelism' and 'social action' but about a biblical way of dealing with people:

Niger, 2004: Hadija, a 15-year-old nomadic girl, is baptised in the desert. Her decision brought opposition from within her tribe: 'My friends say that I am bad, that I am doing wrong by following Jesus. But God has given me happiness and joy.' Hadija first heard about Jesus through Tearfund partner Jemed, which helped resettle her family when drought forced them from the desert to Niger's capital city Niamey.

My analogy was that parents concerned for their children want to make sure they are well fed and go to a decent school, and if they're Christians they want to make sure they grow up knowing Jesus. The one way a parent could be guaranteed to bring up a child who did not want to know Jesus would be to only ever read Bible stories at bedtime

Challenge

❝ There was that very early Tearfund slogan, 'They can't eat prayer', which in its time I guess must have been quite scandalous in some circles of evangelicalism. Yet it communicated very powerfully that it is important to pray but it is also important to do. It put that faith and action thing together in a way that must have seemed incredibly brash and provocative and yet brought a challenge. I think the fact that it brought that challenge not in a foolhardy way but backed up with really good theology and really good people gave it a credibility that cut through.

I think the challenge before us now is the issue of personal lifestyle discipleship. It's not enough to campaign against injustice or global warming if our lifestyles are actually contributing to injustice and global warming on a personal level. We have had a blind spot concerning what the Bible teaches about creation and stewardship, but it's the poor that suffer and pay the price for our lifestyles. Tearfund has got to be very prophetic about that and keep challenging the church. ❞

David Westlake, Tearfund 1996–

Support

❝ I have known Tearfund since early 1984 and I'm convinced by its philosophy and beliefs. For me Tearfund is *the* evangelical organisation that supports the local church, that does advocacy, that does relief, that serves the church in the world. And its impact is huge in our country. We wouldn't be where we are today if we were not in partnership with Tearfund. ❞

Philippe Ouedraogo, Director, AEAD, Burkina Faso

and never feed them. If you love people you want them to develop fully in body, mind and spirit, and for a Christian that full development includes coming to know Christ.

Evangelism without social action is bad evangelism, and social action without evangelism is bad social action, because if you try to preach the gospel to people but don't show any practical interest in their physical needs, why would they want to listen to that gospel?

As the 1990s progressed, Tearfund made a concerted effort to establish a clear theological understanding of what made its work specifically Christian and distinctive: What was the essence of Christian development?

Looking back, it is possible to see that by the grace of God and with many years of work, Tearfund saw two achievements that at one time in its history might have seemed mutually exclusive. The first is that it established itself as a credible, professional organisation, respected in its field. The second is that it held true to its founding values, remaining a thoroughly and distinctively Christian organisation. As Doug Balfour put it during his time as General Director, Tearfund's motivating goal was 'spiritual passion and professional excellence'.

The professional excellence became evident as Tearfund increased its dealings with the wider world of development and emergency relief, but if anything this increased the risk that the organisation would compromise its Christian conviction and motivation. Tearfund therefore

Opposite: Guatemala, 2002: Pedro Par and his family give thanks for their food. In a poor rural area where malnutrition is a major issue, Tearfund's partner the Life Association helped families like Pedro's grow nourishing vegetables. The family saw change in other areas too when Pedro became a Christian. Life Association's executive director Axel Suquen said, 'We want people to enjoy a good relationship with God, and then to create their own community projects, make their own dreams and carry them out. We want them to have abundant life, as Jesus promised, to have peace with God, with creation, and with other people.'

Mission

❝ As disciples of Christ we are called to 'integral mission'. For me, this means I do my level best to bear witness that Christ is Lord of my whole life, twenty-four hours a day, seven days a week. And how do I bear witness? Well, it's through what I say, what I do, how I live, how I relate to others, what I live for, what I am. ❞

Matthew Frost, Tearfund 2005–

pursued a parallel course of exploring and defining its Christian foundations, the result of which was the development in 1996 of its *Operating principles*.

Dewi Hughes was one of the team that worked on this project:

> We wanted to be sure we were not just adopting secular methods and baptising them with the Bible, but instead developing a biblical world-view. It was amazing to have theologians and development people sitting down to talk and listen, drawing out a set of principles which are

Rwanda, 1995: Months after the Rwandan genocide which turned neighbour against neighbour in a cruel slaughter, Tearfund's partner African Revival Ministries brought divided communities together to rebuild homes – and at the same time to build reconciliation.

Part

❝ I think it's fantastic that we've got this organisation constantly reminding the church that there is an alternative to the self-centred consumerist life.

We've had Tearfund just telling people all the time that the poor are there, that Christian people are expressing the love of Christ towards them, and that you can be part of it. ❞

Dewi Hughes, Tearfund 1987–

thoroughly biblical and thoroughly developmental in a really integrated sort of way.

To me it has been exciting to be part of an organisation which is prepared to learn. As Christians we should be in a continual process of learning, because hopefully we are understanding God's Word more and more from day to day.

Drawing on the experience of development professionals, theologians and Tearfund's Christian partners, the group put together a vision of what constituted distinctively Christian development. At the heart of this was the recognition that poverty stems ultimately

For Tearfund and its partners working with some of the world's poorest people, the effects of climate change will present major challenges for years to come.

Here to stay

“ Our involvement in issues of poverty and the alleviation of suffering is because of the compassion of our Lord Jesus Christ. We are commanded by God himself to do it. If I don't do it, then I'm irrelevant.

NGOs come and go, but the church is there to stay. And because it is doing this work out of compassion, even if the funds are not there the church will continue to do it. Why? Because that's its calling. ”

Francis Mkandawire, General Secretary, Evangelical Association of Malawi

DNA

❝ I think one of the most important achievements of Tearfund is that for evangelical Christians there is now a general acceptance that Christians will be people who are generous towards the poor. That has become part of the understanding of what a Christian is about.

Someone once said, 'How do you know an evangelical Christian?' The answer was, 'Well, they'll read their Bible, they'll go to church on a Sunday and they'll give to Tearfund.' Tearfund became part of the DNA of what it meant to be a real evangelical Christian. ❞

Stephen Rand, Tearfund 1979–2004

Malawi, 2004: Tearfund's partner the Chisomo Children's Club used drama, music and street-cleaning projects to help street children find self-worth and to change local attitudes towards them.

from broken relationships, and the goal of Christian development was seen as what the Bible called *shalom*: restored relationships with the Creator, with others in the community and with the environment:

The causes of poverty and marginalisation are complex, but we believe they stem from broken relationships. The goal of Christian development is restored relationships with the Creator, with others in

community and with the environment. The world God made was good, but human rebellion has led to exclusion, mistrust, greed and injustice. Jesus Christ came in the fulfilment of the promise of God to restore good relationships between God, his people and creation. Through the incarnation, death and resurrection of Christ, people are saved from God's condemnation. They become part of God's new community and experience the peace and justice of his coming rule. God has a special concern for the poor and pow-

> **H**e has shown all you people what is good. And what does the Lord require of you? To act justly and to love mercy and to walk humbly with your God. (Micah 6:8)

erless. Because God's intention is reconciliation and community he has a special concern for those who are marginalised and excluded.

The peace and justice of God's kingdom are recognisable now through the power of the Holy Spirit, but will only be fully realised when Christ returns in glory. In the power of the Holy Spirit we are called to play our part in bringing reconciliation to our disordered world. Tearfund's focus is on the economically poor and powerless, but our concern is to see restored relationships in all their fullness, not just economic well-being.

Christian development is distinctive because of our commitment to reconciling people to God. However, in the Bible, reconciliation with God cannot be separated from reconciliation with others. Our responsibility to God is expressed through our response to others. This is the well-spring of Christian development.

The *Operating principles* identified the characteristics of Christian development. They presented a model of Christians reflecting the

Distinctive

❝ I feel that Tearfund's Christian distinctiveness comes out of a real understanding of some of the great prophetic and visionary passages in the Bible. We are called to be workers in the vineyard, to help to bring in the kingdom of God, and that's what it is about. The kingdom of God is here, yet it is also still to come – but we see in the Bible a picture of what God's best for people is – as Isaiah says, living at peace in their own homes and enjoying their own crops. We won't see it all in our lives, but we know that in the end God will intervene and will bring in his kingdom. That's what drives me. That's my vision. That is what I believe. ❞

Jennie Collins, Tearfund 1992–2000

The church as a prayerful, worshipping community expressing the love and compassion of God to those around it is at the heart of Tearfund's vision for transformation.

love and compassion of Christ for people in need, aiming to be like him in everything they do, and practising accountability, transparency and mutual trust:

> The New Testament gives little explicit teaching on either evangelistic or developmental methods. Instead it calls upon the church to be a caring, inclusive and distinctive community of reconciliation reaching out in love to the world. When we see the church in this way there is no opposition between evangelism and social action.

In this model, Christian development is characterised by servant leadership and includes people, especially the marginalised and excluded, in decisions that affect their lives. Recognising the dignity God has given people, it empowers them to have a voice, to make choices and become agents of change. It works with the whole community, addressing their needs

No fear

❝ Now I don't fear the future, because I rely on God and I've learnt how to provide food for my family. ❞
Sarah Nchoe, Maasai mother, Kenya

Demonstration

❝ We can go out and tell people that Jesus is the Saviour and that if they accept Jesus they will go to heaven, but we are talking to widows, to people with AIDS, to orphans, to elderly people, to people who don't know how to read and write, to people who don't have clean water. So for us in AEAD integral mission means combining our spiritual message with meeting the physical needs of the people. It's about making sure that any Christian or local group or church can take the faith they have in Jesus Christ and demonstrate it practically within their community. ❞
Philippe Ouedraogo, Director, AEAD, Burkina Faso

in a sustainable way so that positive change becomes a continuing process.

The context for all this is identified as prayer:

> In all that we do we are totally dependent on God. There is a spiritual reality to development which a secular worldview often ignores. We are engaged in a spiritual conflict. Therefore prayer is essential for Christian development. The only way to keep going and see significant change is through the gracious power and presence of the Holy Spirit.

Tearfund's partner the Meserete Kristos Church has brought education for the first time to poor and remote communities in Ethiopia. It started literacy classes because few people could read the Bible, but then local people asked the church to help them set up schools for 2,500 children. Kume, 13 (pictured centre), said, 'Before you have an education, how can you think about the future?'

The *Operating principles* also stressed the central role of the local church:

> The church is central to God's saving purpose. It is the community in which God lives by his Spirit... Sustainable Christian development requires sustainable Christian communities.

As Tim Chester, another member of the group, put it,

> The text of the gospel message is set in the context of our actions and our lives and the life of the Christian community together.

In 1999, Tearfund was instrumental in the creation of the Micah Network, an international network of some 300 evangelical Christian relief, development and justice agencies. Two years later, the Micah Network convened 140 leaders of Christian organisations involved with the poor from fifty countries to reflect on their mission. One of the fruits of this meeting was a further attempt to explore exactly what made Christian work in this sphere distinctive.

A new term now came to the fore: 'integral mission', borrowed from the Spanish *misión integral*, reflecting something of the indivisible nature of the church's ministry in the earth. The Micah Network consultation issued a declaration which defined it in this way:

> Integral mission or holistic transformation is the proclamation and demonstration of the gospel. It is not simply that evangelism and social involvement are to be done alongside each other. Rather, in integral mission our proclamation has social consequences as we call people to love and repentance in all areas of life. And our social involvement has evangelistic consequences as we bear witness to the transforming grace of Jesus Christ. If we ignore the world we betray the

Opposite: In arid northeast Brazil, Tearfund partner Ação Evangélica (Acev) works in poor communities and has a vision to see every aspect of people's lives transformed by the gospel. They dig wells for villages that have no water, provide small business loans, run schools and a Bible college, provide healthcare, plant churches and speak out against injustice. Their work has gained them respect in the community. As one of Acev's local pastors says, 'We're doing it because that's what we believe Christians should do. It's seen as something practical; we're not swapping it for the gospel, but we're doing it as an expression of what Christianity is.'

Quality

❝ We believe in empowering the church so it can do its work. This is very important. During all the years of war in southern Sudan people went through a lot of suffering, but there was tremendous growth in the church. I am excited by this growth, but I will be much more excited when it is not just in terms of quantity but also in quality. ❞
Anthony Poggo, Executive Director, Across, Sudan

Tearfund believes the goal of Christian development work is restored relationships with God, with other people and with the environment.

word of God which sends us out to serve the world. If we ignore the word of God we have nothing to bring to the world. Justice and justification by faith, worship and political action, the spiritual and the material, personal change and structural change belong together. As in the life of Jesus, being, doing and saying are at the heart of our integral task.

Local church

Our understanding of the causes and cures of poverty from a biblical perspective leads us to believe that there is a central role for Christians outworking integral mission in the context of the local church. That is how poverty is overcome at a local level.
Matthew Frost, Tearfund 2005–

In the light of this, Tearfund's work with poor people was seen as part of the continuing transforming engagement of Christ with the world through his church. His lordship extended to every aspect of life. As René Padilla, Tearfund's International President from 1998 to 2007, put it in a paper for a Micah Network consultation on globalisation in 2003,

> If Jesus Christ is Lord of the universe, his sovereignty includes the economic as well as the political sphere, the social as well as the cultural, the aesthetic as well as the ecological, the personal as well as the societal. Nothing and nobody are outside the sphere of his lordship. It follows that if Jesus Christ is Lord of all and everyone, the Church is not simply an agent for 'individual salvation' that puts the benefits of Christ's work within the reach of people, but the community called to embody the witness to his lordship over the totality of life. Whoever hears the Gospel and responds positively, by so doing becomes a follower of Jesus – he or she then begins a transformation process which lasts throughout life and involves every aspect of life…

> Jesus' disciples will not be distinct because they are mere adherents to a religion – a 'Jesus cult,' so to say – but because they follow a lifestyle that reflects the love and the justice of the Kingdom of God. The mission of the Church, therefore, cannot be restricted to 'saving souls' and 'planting churches' – her mission is to make disciples who learn to obey the Lord in all circumstances of daily life, in private as well as in the public matters, in the spiritual as well as in the material sphere. The call of the Gospel is a call to a holistic transformation which will reflect God's purpose to redeem his creation in all its dimensions – a transformation based on the whole Gospel centred in the Lord

Impact

I still meet people who, when they hear that I used to work for Tearfund, say, 'Oh, Tearfund – they gave me my first break, they gave me my first scholarship, they gave me my first grant, they got us started on this.' Tearfund seems to have had a huge role in helping local Christian leaders in the two-thirds world to get started in terms of entering the social action arena and having a voice and input in their own countries.
Doug Balfour, Tearfund 1995–2004

Catalyst

❝ I think Tearfund has had a special catalytic role, given to it by God. It has had a massive catalytic effect on evangelical Christians in the UK and around the world. It started with George Hoffman giving a clarion call and it has changed the way evangelicals think about social action. There are many Christian organisations today that owe a debt of gratitude to Tearfund and to what God did through it: what they do is only possible because of the theological change that happened back then. ❞

Doug Balfour, Tearfund 1995–2004

In its early days Tearfund stressed its conviction that 'man does not live by bread alone'. It has continued to believe that a biblical approach means meeting people's spiritual as well as material needs, and it works with those who want to introduce people to the life-changing love of Christ.

Jesus Christ and oriented toward the fulfilment of Jesus' desire that his followers be 'the salt of the earth' and 'the light of the world.'

For Dewi Hughes, the vision of Tearfund and the church-based groups it works with around the world is ultimately one of discipleship:

Tearfund depends on donations from individuals, families and churches for most of its income, and supporters have a long tradition of inventive fundraising. In 2005, student Sam Wakeling raised £2,500 by unicycling from Land's End to John O'Groats.

I would say that integral mission is the task of working through the lordship of Jesus Christ in the whole of our life. Our calling as Christians to serve the poor, which is a clear biblical calling to us as individuals and as the church, is part of that whole huge picture. As for Tearfund, as an organisation we have a specific calling to stir up gifts of good works, of caring for the poor.

We do Christian development because we love Christ, and that's a very distinctive thing. We're not content if people have improved physical circumstances: that is not the be all and end all for us. We are only content if people know the blessing of God

But you, God, see the trouble of the afflicted; you consider their grief and take it in hand. The victims commit themselves to you; you are the helper of the fatherless. (Psalm 10:14)

Following Jesus

We at Ação Evangélica (Acev) work with poor people in the endemic drought region of north-east Brazil, drilling wells, improving people's goat and sheep flocks, planting drought-resistant trees, helping people with loans to create income, and so on. We don't see these activities as separate from our evangelism, church-planting and Bible teaching, any more than Jesus did. It's all part of following Jesus. Didn't Jesus teach and preach, as well as heal and feed the hungry?

So when we work with communities, we don't go in saying, 'You want a well? Well then, you've got to have a church with it!' That would be just as corrupt as politicians buying votes, which we find a lot here. In fact, we warn susceptible voters against this. However, we are sure that God's love is revealed through preaching *and* demonstrating his love practically. We have often seen it have wonderful, positive and life-transforming effects.

John Medcraft, Director, Ação Evangélica, Brazil

in all its fullness, in the sense of *shalom*, knowing God, and knowing his peace in their lives and his provision for them.

We've hung on to that original core idea, 'They can't eat prayer', and Tearfund is still very much appealing to people's compassion and telling how our Christian partners show Christ's compassion. It is the heart of what we are about.

As Tearfund prepared to enter its fifth decade, it was thus emboldened by a clear vision and a fresh excitement about what God would do in and through his church worldwide. In 2006 the organisation drew up a strategy for the next ten years, affirming its commitment to integral mission as a biblical model for Christian mission and discipleship. Central to this strategy was the unique role of the local church as 'a global movement with the presence, influence and resources to tackle poverty both spiritually and materially'. Tearfund affirmed its commitment to work in partnership with local churches around the world as they reach out to those who are materially poor in their communities, expressing God's love in practical, sacrificial, visible discipleship. According to Matthew Frost,

Our vision is to see 50 million people lifted out of extreme poverty by 2016, their lives and communities transformed through the work and witness of Christians and local churches. And so we would like to see a global movement of more than 100,000 local churches that is united, prophetic and influential, bringing hope to people living in poverty,

Passionate

❝ We are Christians passionate about the local church bringing justice and transforming lives – overcoming global poverty. And so our vision is to see 50 million people released from material and spiritual poverty through a worldwide network of 100,000 local churches. ❞
Praying for a miracle, Tearfund, 2007

and here in the UK and Ireland a million Christians who are committed to lives of radical discipleship and integral mission. As Christians, we are passionate about the local church bringing justice and transforming lives – overcoming global poverty.

For Matthew, the path that Tearfund has travelled since 1968 is remarkable:

As Tearfund enters its fifth decade, its vision is still to see people released from material and spiritual poverty.

I am really struck by the way the foundation of Tearfund was really showered in prayer. There was the sense that everything was done through the lens of prayer first. We had almost no resources, we were not a professional organisation, but everything was done in reliance on God. As you look at much of the early success, you think it was only possible because God clearly intervened in some way. Now we've grown into an organisation of 1,000 people worldwide which has accomplished enormous amounts and has a very clear vision and calling for the future.

This is not an organisation that has had to compromise its faith in God and make sacrifices in order to become a professional development agency. There is a stake planted firmly in the ground that says this is who we are: we are an organisation that is passionate about seeing God's kingdom come, and that is the context for everything else that follows. That stake has never been moved: it is still where it has always been.

Just as in its earliest days, Tearfund continues to support the work of Christians in the poorest parts of the world as they make the love of God a tangible reality for people in need. The fruit continues too: bringing poor people clean water, education, health, income, justice, and the opportunity to know the God who has made it possible and who wants them to taste life as he intended it.

There is no way to measure how many lives have been changed as a result of the existence of Tearfund. It can safely be said, however, that they are numbered in millions. Through the faithful prayer, giving and work of Tearfund's supporters and the sacrificial service of its Christian partners throughout the world, the fullness of life that Jesus promised has become a reality for countless people who otherwise would not have known it.

David White became chairman of Tearfund's board in 1999, fired by the same enthusiasm for Tearfund's vision that had motivated

What good is it, my brothers and sisters, if people claim to have faith but have no deeds? Can such faith save them? Suppose a brother or sister is without clothes and daily food. If one of you says to them, 'Go in peace; keep warm and well fed,' but does nothing about their physical needs, what good is it? In the same way, faith by itself, if it is not accompanied by action, is dead. But someone will say, 'You have faith; I have deeds.' Show me your faith without deeds, and I will show you my faith by what I do. (James 2:14–18)

For millions of people living in poverty – like Azeta, a wife and mother in Burkina Faso – life is a daily challenge. Azeta and her family were helped to grow more food by Tearfund's local church partner. Azeta said: 'When you have children and there isn't enough rainfall, you are worried. But the God who created us will take care of us.'

him to be involved for twenty years as a volunteer. As David looked back – and forward – in 2007, the challenge of the future was huge and yet inspiring:

> In a world confronted by extreme poverty, injustice, the AIDS pandemic, climate change, disease and disasters, the needs are enormous, but we know God wants us to rise to these challenges.

Zambia, 2001: As HIV spread insidiously through communities, Tearfund's partner the Evangelical Fellowship of Zambia mobilised an army of church volunteers to visit the sick, bringing comfort and practical help. Leah Mutala (pictured praying with women whose grown-up children have died) told the volunteers, 'We are doing this as though Jesus Christ was here: we become his hands and his presence.'

The Spirit of the Lord is on me, because he has anointed me to proclaim good news to the poor. He has sent me to proclaim freedom for the prisoners and recovery of sight for the blind, to set the oppressed free, to proclaim the year of the Lord's favour. (Luke 4:18–19)

The great thing about Tearfund is that it was born out of a groundswell of concern among God's people. It wasn't just dreamed up as a good idea: it was a move of God among his people. The Lord was speaking and something was bound to come of it – in God's grace it happened to be Tearfund.

As we look to the future, we want to see the world changed as people proclaim, live and put into practical action the gospel in all its fullness. We know we are a part of the church and we go in the name of the church. We believe that the greatest need of poor people is to find peace with God, and that the way people find peace with God is through Christ alone – that is why we only partner with those who want to introduce the people they serve to Christ. That is our distinctiveness.

I believe Tearfund's calling today is what it has always been: to see the Kingdom of God extended and the name of Christ uplifted, to see people experiencing the love of Christ, his justice and his peace.

In 1968 Tearfund started a revolution. Its story is not yet over.